New Collec

EAVAN BOLAND was born in Dubl
1967. In 1994 she was poet in residenc
in Dublin. She has received numerous awards for her writing. She is
Mabury Knapp Professor at Stanford University where she is director of
the Creative Writing Program. She divides her time between California and
Dublin where she lives with her husband, the novelist Kevin Casey.

ı

Also by Eavan Boland from Carcanet Press

Poetry
Night Feed
The Journey
Selected Poems
Outside History
In a Time of Violence
The Lost Land
Code

Prose
Object Lessons

EAVAN BOLAND

New Collected Poems

CARCANET

Acknowledgements

23 Poems was first published in 1962 by Gallagher Press, Dublin; *New Territory* in 1967 by Allen Figgis, Dublin; *The War Horse* in 1975 by Gollancz, London; *In Her Own Image* in 1980 by Arlen House, Dublin.

03928224

First published in Great Britain in 2005 by
Carcanet Press Limited
Alliance House
Cross Street
Manchester M2 7AQ

Copyright © Eavan Boland 1962, 1967, 1975, 1980, 1987, 1990, 1994, 1998, 2001, 2005

A CIP catalogue record for this book is available from the British Library
ISBN 1 85754 858 2

The publisher acknowledges financial assistance from Arts Council England

Typeset by XL Publishing Services, Tiverton
Printed and bound in England by SRP Ltd, Exeter

Contents

In Her Own Image   1980

Night Feed   1980

The Journey   1987

I

II

Outside History   1990

In a Time of Violence   1994

The Lost Land   1998

Code   2001

For Kevin, Sarah and Eavan Frances

Author's Note

All the poems from nine volumes of poetry have been collected here. Nothing has been left out. Edits and exclusions from the *Selected Poems* have been reversed. The two volumes that the *Collected Poems* of 1995 did not include – *The Lost Land* and *Code* – have been added. In addition, I have retrieved two poems from *23 Poems*, a chapbook which came out in 1962 when I was eighteen. I have also added a brief section from an unpublished verse play, part of which appeared in the *Irish Press* in 1971 under the title 'Femininity and Freedom'.

from 23 POEMS
1962

Liffeytown

Liffey, tawny and asleep in the browsing dusk,
Clings to the dark, enchanted ovals
Of the bridge.
O swan by swan my heart goes down
Through Dublin town, through Dublin town.

Single and bestowing they wander in the olive water,
Dragging a shaft of light behind them in the drowse
Of the evening.
O swan by swan my heart goes down
Through Dublin town, through Dublin town.

Ghosting shadows in the gloom of Liffeytown,
They weave their quiet spell upon the darkening
Of the river.
O swan by swan my heart goes down
Through Dublin town, through Dublin town.

The Liffey beyond Islandbridge

Past town, the Liffey breaks from iron into grass,
Then wanders, with the swans preening
In the shaken warmth of early March
And white abandoned sea birds leaning
On the wind. A cat steps cautiously
Among the daffodils. Under a tree
An old man contemplates his shoe,
Or turns to what he never thought to see
Again, the water fretted by a cygnet's thrust.
Look well. Further beyond that river bend
Are spaces teemed with cities which must
Strike a destiny. But here for aimless miles
The river flattens to the land.

NEW TERRITORY
1967

FOR MY MOTHER

A word, a solitary word tells all, and that word is love.   Yeats

The Poets

They, like all creatures, being made
For the shovel and worm,
Ransacked their perishable minds and found
Pattern and form
And with their own hands quarried from hard words
A figure in which secret things confide.

They are abroad: their spirits like a pride
Of lions circulate,
Are desperate, just as the jewelled beast,
That lion constellate,
Whose scenery is Betelgeuse and Mars,
Hunts without respite among fixed stars.

And they prevail: to his undoing every day
The essential sun
Proceeds, but only to accommodate
A tenant moon,
And he remains until the very break
Of morning, absentee landlord of the dark.

The Gryphons

From Greek hearsay
Comes the story of a man
Who begged for deathless life and lived to pay
For it in tears, when
From his golden head, his body's pride
The energy retreated, and then died.

These ugly creatures
Without asking are awarded
Fairer terms: their nightmare granite features
Will be saved and hoarded,
While around them in the timely night
Falter our brief extremities of light.

The story goes
That when he saw his body die
And he lived on, he dried his tears, arose
And stared into the sky:
'No one but I,' he shouted, 'on this earth
Knows that the very dearest thing is death.'

He was released,
But how do these perennial stones
Endure the prospect of a living feast?
No one can hear their groans
Nor offer them a respite – we can at most
Find in the granite eyes a fierce request.

The Pilgrim

for Eamon Grennan

When the nest falls in winter, birds have flown
To distant lights and hospitality.
The pilgrim, with his childhood home a ruin,
Shares their fate and, like them, suddenly
Becomes a tenant of the wintry day.
Looking back, out of the nest of stone
As it tumbles, he can see his childhood
Flying away like an evicted bird.

Underground although the ground is bare,
Summer is turning on her lights. Spruce
And larch and massive chestnut will appear
Above his head in leaf. Oedipus
Himself, cold and sightless, was aware
Of no more strife or drama at Colonus:
He became, when he could go no further,
Just an old man hoping for warm weather.

At journey's end in the waters of a shrine,
No greater thing will meet him than the shock
Of his own human face, beheaded in
The holy pool. Steadily he must look
At this unshriven thing among the bells
And offerings, and for his penance mark
How his aspiring days like fallen angels
Follow one another into the dark.

New Territory

Several things announced the fact to us:
The captain's Spanish tears
Falling like doubloons in the headstrong light,
And then of course the fuss –
The crew jostling and interspersing cheers
With wagers. Overnight
As we went down to our cabins, nursing the last
Of the grog, talking as usual of conquest,
Land hove into sight.

Frail compasses and trenchant constellations
Brought us as far as this,
And now air and water, fire and earth
Stand at their given stations
Out there, and are ready to replace
This single desperate width
Of ocean. Why do we hesitate? Water and air
And fire and earth and therefore life are here,
And therefore death.

Out of the dark man comes to life and into it
He goes and loves and dies,
(His element being the dark and not the light of day)
So the ambitious wit
Of poets and exploring ships have been his eyes –
Riding the dark for joy –
And so Isaiah of the sacred text is eagle-eyed because
By peering down the unlit centuries
He glimpsed the holy boy.

Mirages

At various times strenuous sailing men
Claim to have seen creatures of myth
Scattering light at the furthest points of dawn –

Creatures too seldom seen to reward the patience
Of a night-watch, who provide no ready encore
But like the stars revisit generations.

And kings riding to battle on the advice
Of their ambition have seen crosses burn
In the skylight of the winter solstice.

Reasonable men, however, hold aloof,
Doubting the gesture, speech and anecdote
Of those who touch the Grail and bring no proof –

Failing to recognise that in their fast
Ethereal way, mirages are
This daylight world in summary and forecast.

So a prince, a fledgling still and far
From coronation, kept at home,
Will draw his sword and murder empty air –

And should his father die and that death bring
Him majesty, his games have been his school,
His phantom war a forcing house of kings.

Migration

for Michael Longley

From August they embark on every wind,
Managing with grace
This new necessity, widely determined
On a landing place.
Daredevil swallows, coloured swifts go forth
Like some great festival removing south.

Cuckoo and operatic nightingale
Meeting like trains of thought
Concluding summer, in complete agreement, file
Towards the sea at night,
And find at last their bright geometry
(Triumphant overland) is not seaworthy.

Sandpiper, finch and wren and goldencrest,
Whose baffled
Movements start or finish summer, now at last
Return, single and ruffled,
And lift up their voices in a world of light,
And choose their loves as though determined to forget.

As though upon their travels, as each bird
Fell down to die, the sea
Had opened, showing those above a graveyard
Without sanctity –
Birds and their masters, many beautiful,
Tumbled together without name or burial.

The Dream of Lir's Son

extract from a narrative

'I saw a country tree as green as grass
Clasp the simple daylight in its boughs
Like love; at last it swelled with fruit
And to its fertile house a bird brought
Its house, and sang aloud in leafy splendour
Until my ears were dazed at its air,
My human eyes dazzled at its lodging.
Day was darkening as I stood watching,
Suddenly I watched by moonlight. Time
Stopped: my old sweet nurse, that light was autumn
Without time's assent; it stripped bare
The tree, shrivelling its leaves, its fair
Fruit, and only spared the bird to sing
Who sang in the clipped boughs till, wondering,
I woke.' 'I tell, you, you were better',
His nurse answered him, 'to hold this matter
Close and keep it light, for there are times
Indeed when in secret forms, dreams
Mime and play the future's mystery
Before the present; but in the main, merely
They are jackanapes of yesterday, full
of nothing, just as after nursery school
When you were young and naughty, your good pocket
Would be filled with snails and twine, picked
As treasure by your childish brain and worthless,
And the weary mind makes no wiser choice
Asleep.'

Malediction

from 'The Son of Lir'

Son of Lir as lonely are you now
As the leaf when lightning strikes the tree
And the bird when thunder breaks his bough.
Now is lost, as bird and leaf and tree
Son of Lir, your humanity.

Now the steady shoulders, the bright arms
You opened wide for battle and love's sake –
Encumbered to white wings by my charms –
Must beat the air and the air must break
With your human heart, your tender neck.

The seed of man is barren in this body!
The wit of man abandons this cursed brain!
The blood of man turns back and flows muddy
From this changing heart, and this fair skin
Is ruffling in the feathers of a swan.

I take your youth under magic seizure.
Farewell the joy of summer in a field;
Farewell the simple seasons and their pleasure;
Farewell true gold and the silk worm's yield:
Son of Lir I banish you this world

To know the flinching cold of seas which spring
Forgets, whose branch is ice, whose flower is snow
And where the wild dead lie wintering
Forever.

Lullaby

from a narrative poem

O nurse, when I was a rascal boy, bold
February winds were snaffling gold
Out of the crocuses; there in grief
For the pretty, gaudy things I'd cry: 'Stop thief'
And you would grumble: 'Child, let be, let be.'
Or we would come across a sapling tree
To discover frost sipping its new blood;
I'd join my arms around its perished wood
And weep, and you would say: 'Now child, its place
Is in a merry hearth, not your embrace.'
And one April morning that was filled
With mating tunes, a nest of finches spilled
Which slipped its flowering anchor in a gale.
I cupped one in my fingers, dead and small.
But late that night you stole to me on tiptoe
And whispered: 'Child, child, the winds must blow.'

Belfast vs Dublin

for Derek Mahon

Into this city of largesse
You carried clever discontent,
And now, the budget of your time here spent,
Let us not mince the word: this is no less
Than halfway towards the end. Gathering
In a rag tied to a stick, all in confusion,
Dublin reverence and Belfast irony –
Now hoist with your conclusion.

Cut by the throats before we spoke
One to another, yet we breast
The dour line of North and South, pressed
Into action by the clock. Here we renounce
All dividend except the brilliant quarrel
Of our towns: mine sports immoral
Courtiers in unholy waste, but your unwitty
Secret love for it is Belfast city.

We have had time to talk, and strongly
Disagree about the living out
Of life. There was no need to shout.
Rightly or else quite wrongly
We have run out of time, if not of talk.
Let us then cavalierly fork
Our ways, since we, and all unknown,
Have called into question one another's own.

Requiem for a Personal Friend

on a half-eaten blackbird

A striped philistine with quick
Sight, quiet paws, today –
In gorging on a feathered prey –
Filleted our garden's music.

Such robbery in such a mouthful!
Here rests, shovelled under simple
Vegetables, my good example –
Singing daily, daily faithful.

No conceit and not contrary –
My best colleague, worst of all,
Was half-digested, his sweet whistle
Swallowed like a dictionary.

Little victim, song for song –
Who share a trade must share a threat –
So I write to cheat the cat
Who got your body, of my tongue.

A Cynic at Kilmainham Gaol

for Connie Neenan

There is nowhere that the gimlet twilight has not
Entered, not a thing indeed to see,
But it is excellent abroad for ghosts:
A gaslamp in the dark seems to make sea
Water in the rising fog – maybe
For those imprisoned here this was a small
Consoling inland symbol – how could their way be
Otherwise discovered back to the western sea-board?
How could they otherwise be free in prison
Who for more than forty years have been shot through
To their Atlantic hearts?
                              But in this wizened
Autumn dark, no worship, mine or yours
Can resurrect the sixteen minds. O those,
Perhaps (Godspeed them) saw the guns with dual
Sight – seeing from one eye with the tears they chose
Themselves the magic, tragic town, the broken
Countryside, the huge ungenerous tribe
Of cowards – and the one eye laughing saw
(God help them) growing from their own graves to jibe
At death, a better future, neither tear nor flaw.

From the Painting Back From Market *by Chardin*

Dressed in the colours of a country day –
Grey-blue, blue-grey, the white of seagulls' bodies –
Chardin's peasant woman
Is to be found at all times in her short delay
Of dreams, her eyes mixed
Between love and market, empty flagons of wine
At her feet, bread under her arm. He has fixed
Her limbs in colour, and her heart in line.

In her right hand, the hindlegs of a hare
Peep from a cloth sack; through the door
Another woman moves
In painted daylight; nothing in this bare
Closet has been lost
Or changed. I think of what great art removes:
Hazard and death, the future and the past,
This woman's secret history and her loves –

And even the dawn market, from whose bargaining
She has just come back, where men and women
Congregate and go
Among the produce, learning to live from morning
To next day, linked
By a common impulse to survive, although
In surging light they are single and distinct,
Like birds in the accumulating snow.

Shakespeare

for Philip Edwards

You wrote because you had to. Sycophants
And merchant seamen crowded in, siblings
Of the court made the whole age a performance,
With the plague waiting in the wings.

You wrote because you had to. Every line
Was sack and supper for yourself and Burbage;
New Place and the status Gentleman
Were both the tragic and the comic wage.

You wrote because of loneliness, London,
Hunger to begin with. When like the Thames
You saw your life flow downwards towards its loss,

You made of every quill the fire which men
Primitively lit against the beasts, whose flames
Were agile sentries between them and chaos.

The Comic Shakespeare

Legend has you holding horses' heads,
Standing for pennies at their heads in rain,
Collecting skills, finally playing leads
In the provinces, fingering your pen.

Those years are lost. Looking for them later,
You – apprentice turned chameleon –
Use comic disguise. Your youth, like water
Hopelessly dispersed, has become

Princes, clowns, improbable situations –
Facile cleansing through false jeopardy.
Were such bright, primary solutions
Born of brightness? Would each comedy,

Each festival and whistle of your prime,
Today exist if you had wept in time?

Yeats in Civil War

Presently a strange thing happened:
I began to smell honey in places
where honey could not be.

In middle age you exchanged the sandals
Of a pilgrim for a Norman keep
In Galway. Civil war started, vandals
Sacked your country, made off with your sleep;

Somehow you arranged your escape
Aboard a spirit-ship which every day
Hoisted sail out of fire and rape,
And on that ship your mind was stowaway.

The sun mounted on a wasted place,
But the wind at every door and turn
Blew the smell of honey in your face
Where there was none. Whatever we may learn

You are its sum, struggling to survive –
A fantasy of honey your reprieve.

The Flight of the Earls

for Brendan Kennelly

Princes it seems are seldom wise:
Most of them fall for a woman's tears
Or else her laughter, such as Paris
Whose decision stretched to ten alarming years –
Nothing would suit
Until he'd brought
The kingdom down around his ears.

Now in the middle ages see
The legendary boy of king and queen:
A peacock of all chivalry,
He dies at twenty on some battle-green
And ever since
The good Black Prince
Rides to the land of might-have-been.

Whether our own were foolish or wise
Hardly concerns us; death ran away with our chances
Of a meeting, yet we strain our eyes
Hoping perhaps just one with his golden flounces
Has outwitted theft.
So are we left
Writing to headstones and forgotten princes.

After the Irish of Egan O'Rahilly

Without flocks or cattle or the curved horns
Of cattle, in a drenching night without sleep,
My five wits on the famous uproar
Of the wave toss like ships,
And I cry for boyhood, long before
Winkle and dogfish had defiled my lips.

O if he lived, the prince who sheltered me,
And his company who gave me entry
On the river of the Laune,
Whose royalty stood sentry
Over intricate harbours, I and my own
Would not be desolate in Dermot's country.

Fierce McCarthy Mor whose friends were welcome.
McCarthy of the Lee, a slave of late,
McCarthy of Kanturk whose blood
Has dried underfoot:
Of all my princes not a single word –
Irrevocable silence ails my heart.

My heart shrinks in me, my heart ails
That every hawk and royal hawk is lost;
From Cashel to the far sea
Their birthright is dispersed
Far and near, night and day, by robbery
And ransack, every town oppressed.

Take warning wave, take warning crown of the sea,
I, O'Rahilly – witless from your discords –
Were Spanish sails again afloat
And rescue on your tides,
Would force this outcry down your wild throat,
Would make you swallow these Atlantic words.

The King and the Troubadour

for David Norris

A troubadour once lost his king
Who took a carven lute
And crossed the world and tuned its heart
To hear it sing.

Starved, wasted, worn, lost,
His lute his one courage,
He sang his youth to fumbling age,
Fresh years to frost.

In bitter spells his king lay bound
In bitter magic walled;
Within a cruel shape swelled
Love no sound,

No sight, no troubadour searching
Could set free. Fiercely
Came he singing finally
'My king, my king.'

To the window the king's head
Came. The troubadour
Dashed his lute on leaf and flower
And tumbled dead,

And the king at one glance
Seeing ransom ruined,
Majesty perplexed, pined
In magic silence.

The rain of God gathering
Surrounded the smashed lute,
Solving its fragmented heart
Into spring.

The king who in a cruel husk
Of charms became as tragic
Through monotonies of magic
As the dusk,

Each minstrel spring was called and sent
No horrid head, but came
Above the ground, a grassy atom
Hearty as a giant.

Athene's Song

for my father

From my father's head I sprung
Goddess of the war, created
Partisan and soldiers' physic –
My symbols boast and brazen gong –
Until I made in Athens wood
Upon my knees a new music.

When I played my pipe of bone,
Robbed and whittled from a stag,
Every bird became a lover
Every lover to its tone
Found the truth of song and brag;
Fish sprung in the full river.

Peace became the toy of power
When other noises broke my sleep:
Like dreams I saw the hot ranks
And heroes in another flower
Than any there; I dropped my pipe
Remembering their shouts, their thanks.

Beside the water, lost and mute,
Lies my pipe and like my mind
Remains unknown, remains unknown
And in some hollow taking part
With my heart against my hand
Holds its peace and holds its own.

The Winning of Etain

Etain twice a woman twice a queen,
Possessed of two lives and one love,
Twice the loveliest woman ever seen
For whom two kings made Ireland a red grave.
This story tells the winning of Etain
A second time by Aengus, how he strove
To own his own – a tale of tears, of lovers
Lost to each other for a thousand years.

Aengus and Etain lived for each other's pleasure,
With gold for the head of Aengus as a king
And gold so intricate in Etain's hair
No one could guess if the light scattering
Were a woman's beauty or a queen's treasure.
They lived for summer and to dance and sing
But they were doomed when Fergus, the black Druid,
Followed their happiness with fatal hatred.

A summer's night Etain in Aengus's arms
Slept, her head challenging the moon,
Collecting more and more light from beams
Which flared on lovers who would not love again
For a thousand years. All at once the charms
Of Fergus took effect; unlucky Etain,
Warm in Aengus's arms where she lay,
Lost her happiness and lost her joy.

Her cheeks, blanched with light, were charmed away;
Her long embracing arms convulsed; her face
Shrivelled; quick and violent decay
Seized her body and her body's grace
Changed from a queen into a dragon-fly,
Changed to enamelled wings and scales in a space
Of minutes. Then she flew in a glimmer
Away to discover flowers of the summer.

Awakening, Aengus found, instead of Etain,
His arms as empty as a warm nest
Rifled by hawks, and found his love gone,
No hand to kiss, and for his head no breast.
From his window in a summer dawn
Bright as blood, idly he watched the haste
Of birds from branch to branch and below
A dragon-fly sipping at the dew.

Morning danced on its back and decorated
Every scaly tone twice as bright
As hyacinths, above which it waited,
Wings singing, a busy thief of light
And dew. A thousand insect colours scattered
From its body and were deftly caught
By summer flowers like another rain –
And Aengus in that moment cried: 'Etain,

My only love, changed to a brilliant toy
Of sorcery, for you I will compose
A bower of the four seasons and defy
Our new despair: autumn, the year's close,
Summer and spring will tangle for your joy,
The frosty snowdrop twine with the rose,
And January buds with fringed grasses
Where you may stay under my jealous eyes.'

At Aengus's command the thing was done:
Season followed season in his grief,
And from each one a sweet particular crown
Was stolen; bough and petal, fruit and leaf,
Were interwoven for his spellbound queen,
And flowered endlessly about his wife
Who hummed night and day among her many
Suitors, robbing each of dew and honey.

And night and day, Aengus stayed beside,
Asleep or waking, hawking or at rest,
He watched the fertile bower and his bride
Within, but thinking of her white breast,
Her human body in his arms, he cried
Bitterly above the bright twist
Of flowers, but his fast tears were human –
His love, an insect, drank them like the rain.

And still the Druid's hatred followed them,
Redoubled now because they could devise
Happiness within destruction, a form
Of beauty flourishing within disguise.
So he contrived darkness and a storm
Of winds colliding on the fresh seas
To separate the crocus from the rose
And interrupt the dragon-fly's repose.

Suddenly, as Aengus watched, the wind
Tore his green and intricate design
Apart, scattered flowers and unwound
Summer from spring, and autumn's wealthy vine
From winter leaves. He flung his hand
Among stems broken and a rain
Of petals, but the wind swept them towards
The sea where its strength was bred, like birds.

'O Etain, my first love,' Aengus cried,
'Stolen a second time, now who will build
A bower for you over the cold tide?
What blossoms of the country or the field,
What flower or fragrance can the sea provide?
And where will you find dew in the salt
Of the waves? I cast this wretched world behind,
And will not rest until my love is found.'

At his cry, the better powers took pity
On him, loving him because his love
Had once set out to cheat the travesty
Of sorcery and triumphed, but could not save
Etain twice. Invisibility
Was their gift, exemption from the grave –
As well they gave a thousand mortal years
To Aengus and Etain, unlucky lovers.

Like a petal from the flowers sipped
By her on bright days at Aengus's side,
Etain fluttered while the northwind clipped
Her coloured scales and the sea cried
Beneath her. Once she struggled, wings trapped
In the beak of a scavenger, but she escaped
And tossed, a magic atom, on the surface
Of the water, lost in the water's race.

Etain at last baffled and long weary,
Was wildly buffeted, now on a snowy,
Now on a stifling breeze, until clearly
A green and quiet shore began, whose dewy
Grasses sprung out of the wind's way,
And there found flowers in hosts, scarlet and showy
Rivals for her wings, petals to soothe
Her misery and honey for her mouth.

And there she flew above a royal palace
Whose roof, involved and circled like a rose,
Bore mosaics like a clutch of crocuses
And marble whiter than the lily grows.
No wonder then she searched for dew and spice
Among its tiles, mistaking them for flowers,
And tumbled through a cranny, all unseen,
To splash in the bright wine of another queen;

And by that error found another womb,
Another spell of life, another shape,
For the queen lifting up the same
Infested gold cup to her lip
Swallowed insect, wine and all, while the fume
Of the delicate fermented grape
Disguised its tenant. But magic had its way
And worked its charm, and swelled the queen's belly.

Mysteriously she came to be with child,
Another queen, wife of another king
And in another age. She grew heavy and mild.
Contented with the chance, never suspecting
She was fertile from the wine defiled
And not a king's embrace. And so in spring
Was born human, from a magic womb,
Etain into the world a second time.

And so she grew to girlhood, cherishing
All captive things, and grew to hate the forest
Because its horned boughs might be concealing
A bold antelope in charmed arrest,
And wept on summer nights, imagining
The lion howling from his heaven, cased
In stars; but never guessed from where her pity
Sprung, from what unknown captivity.

Where a river rushed into the sea, on a ledge
Of stone, Etain would sit in the evening glow,
Her cheeks as fresh as berries from the hedge,
Her arms white as a single fall of snow,
Her thighs like stems of a flower; and to the edge
Of the water where outrivalled lilies grew,
On a summer night (in every detail the same
As that on which he lost her) Aengus came.

Invisible, he watched her silver comb
Chased with gold, calm her gold hair,
Invisible, he brought to mind a time
When she had bound it back for him with fair
Ornaments which he, when night came,
Unbound again with all a lover's care,
But in another royal life, of
Which nothing remained only love.

'O world,' cried Aengus, 'I have found again
My only love restored to loveliness
For whom I interwove, to catch the sun,
A bower of every blossom, fruit and grass
In each material, from every season
When she was changed by a Druid's malice,
And watched her drink its dew and suck
Its honey, and never realised our luck.

How can I kiss these red forgetful lips,
This unfamiliar hand, or take this body
Which has travelled through so many shapes
Of magic to my side? Can an unready
Girl give back a woman? Can green pips
Sweeten the tongue like fruit, or seedy
Grain be wholesome wheat overnight?
And will I ever find again delight

Which I have searched for a thousand years –
Invisible, but none the less in pain,
And none the less a creature of my tears
Crying at corners of the world "Etain"
Without an answer. And now for all my loss
I must begin to woo my love again.
No arms await me, and no recognition,
Only the chance to win again what's mine.'

Day by summer day Aengus stayed
Beside the cool lake and watched his love
Grow graceful as the forest deer which wade
And drink at dawn, and saw her beauty thrive
And knew she fretted: 'She will be a bride
Before the winter; she for whom I wove
A shelter out of flowers will shelter now
In other arms, and I have lost my labour.'

Out of the South one day a horseman rode,
His head the colour of the harvest corn,
His cloak full, jewelled and embroidered,
A sword weighing at his side, a horn
Curving at his shoulder. There he wooed
Etain while Aengus watched, his heart torn
In two, hearing his love say: 'Yes I will
Give you love for love upon that hill.'

Dawn broke after a fevered night
In cold waves, wide as the sea is deep,
Capsizing the half-moon in tidal light,
But Aengus threw his rival into a sleep
As blind as death and by the dreadful right
Of love, disguised himself within that shape
And climbed the hill alone and there appeared
To Etain as the lover she desired.

All about them acorns and dried leaves
Lay close as gold and silver at a feast,
Friendly trees shaded them like slaves
And the sun rising was their priest,
And even by the hours, usual thieves
Of love, they knew that their embrace was blessed
And Aengus wept, half for simple joy,
Half to be within another body.

Knowing it as the necessary price
Of his possession, yet he felt despair
Because he spoke within another voice,
And kissed with strange lips Etain's fair
Lips, and knew that they were loving twice
In two forms yet with a single fire.
'What would you say, Etain, if you should know
I loved another woman long ago?'

'My only love,' said Etain, 'overhead
Autumn is decking out the chestnut tree
With embers; our cheeks are pressed against dead
Flowers and we have been lovers in a chilly
Womb of snow; but spring will fling a vivid
Colour on this tree and make ready
The world; and with a same difference,
A heart can love again and yet love once.

'Are buds less welcome to the April bough
Because they open where all others have?
Is snow less white, the wingspan of the crow
Less black because their purities survive
From past to future, and from then to now?
And so, is any love not every love?'
And with her words Aengus came to rest
At last, and slept safely on her breast.

With many a trumpet, many a bell's mouth
Opened like a bird's under the sun,
Etain married Conor, king of the South,
Imagining him the lover whe had lain
With her, ignorant of the strange truth,
But very soon discovered to her pain
Her heart was cold, pressed beneath a weight
Like ice, while her love changed to hate.

Bitter words were woven into the stuff
Of disappointment. 'How may I say,' she cried,
'Where love has gone? I loved you well enough
That bold autumn morning on the hillside.'
But Conor turned to her, his speech rough:
'I slept that dawn as though I had been dead.'
Then Etain's heart stirred, her tears
Fell on the stiff frost of a thousand years.

The weather changed; winter with its harsh
Colours became spring; flowers grew,
A stilted crane waded in the marsh,
An argosy of summer fruits blew
Inland on the winds wild and fresh.
Etain only was unstirred by the view
Of the earth waking, but sat alone sewing
Always at her window, always waiting.

Like January's rose to one of June
Her scarlet cheeks dwindled into white,
Her round flesh almost into bone,
The brilliance of her eye became a twilight,
And as the green earth swelled great
With child, she sickened, separate and thin.

May came and the trees were stirred
By blossoms tumbling from their brief stations,
Wrapping the flamboyant grass in a shroud
Like snow, when Etain, sick with long patience,
Saw a figure like a far bird
Enlarge at last and block the summer distance,
And saw a horseman in a rich dress
Drumming across the drawbridge of the palace.

And he was armoured in a suit of seasons:
Flowers of spring adorned his iron greaves;
The icy evergreen, the berry's poisons
Enamelled his wintry visor; flushed leaves
Of autumn inflamed his breast like suns,
And summer was imprinted on his sleeves,
And what with berry, leaf, tree and flower,
He seemed no horseman but a human bower.

And where his lady's token should have been,
A scarf of silk, marked in brilliant paints,
Flapped wildly to the wind's motion,
On which a dragon-fly, seeming at once
To light on every flower, had been drawn.
And Etain from her window knew the prince
For Aengus, and ran to him and took his arm
And mounting up, rode away with him.

from 'FEMININITY AND FREEDOM'

1971

from 'Femininity and Freedom'

Deirdre and Cathal in conversation:

Cathal
The High King, Conchubar, his donkeys weighed
With stones and lockets for your wrists and ears,
Has come himself to woo you in this place.
He bends his knee to you like a raw boy
As if you were not already his by right.

Deirdre
I've seen you steal out of the castle precincts
I've seen you take the river path to the wood
And stood at my window envying your arrival.
You have been walking Cathal, in the wood
While I have risen in my painted chamber
Where my old nurse is puffing round so hard
She lights the fire in the grate so there's no need
For the brass bellows. And I must hear her say
Will it be silk today or the brown damask
And *Deirdre hang a jewel in your ear*
Your eyes are dull and *Deirdre use your palms*
To pummel blood into those pale cheeks
Or the king will think I've sent him down a corpse –
All that time you are in the wood
Crouching by a winter stream whose water
Races across stones too quick for ice.
Or staring through the dusk of a cave where bats
Outsleep the frost in their sightless files.

Cathal
In that wood, Deirdre, there are adders
Coiled at first like bracelets in the grass
Which rear at your approach, strike at your shin
With a startling, fatal tongue. On the twigs are berries
Bunched and innocent as midnight dew
Which in the mouth suddenly strangle breath
And then blacken the face and foul the blood.
Were I a rabbit, Deirdre, when the weasel vampire
Leaps, or a linnet hazarding the hawk
I would think the wood as dangerous a place
As full of snares and monotony as this court.

THE WAR HORSE

1975

.

The Other Woman

for Kevin

I know you have a world I cannot share
Where a woman waits for you, beautiful,
Young no doubt, protected in your care
From stiffening and wrinkling, not mortal

Not shy of her own mirror. How can I rival
Her when like a harem wife she waits
To come into the pages of your novel
Obediently as if to your bed on nights

She is invited; nor as in your other life
I do, reminds you daily of the defeat
Of time, nor as does your other wife
Binds you to the married state?

She is the other woman. I must share
You with her time and time again,
Book after book, yet I am aware
Love, how I have got the better bargain.

For I imagine she has grown strange
To you among the syntax and the sentences
By which you distance her and would exchange
Her speaking part for any of our silences.

The War Horse

This dry night, nothing unusual
About the clip, crop, casual

Iron of his shoes as he stamps death
Like a mint on the innocent coinage of earth.

I lift the window, watch the ambling feather
Of hock and fetlock, loosed from its daily tether

In the tinker camp on the Enniskerry Road,
Pass, his breath hissing, his snuffling head

Down. He is gone. No great harm is done.
Only a leaf of our laurel hedge is torn –

Of distant interest like a maimed limb,
Only a rose which now will never climb

The stone of our house, expendable, a mere
Line of defence against him, a volunteer

You might say, only a crocus its bulbous head
Blown from growth, one of the screamless dead.

But we, we are safe, our unformed fear
Of fierce commitment gone; why should we care

If a rose, a hedge, a crocus are uprooted
Like corpses, remote, crushed, mutilated?

He stumbles on like a rumour of war, huge,
Threatening; neighbours use the subterfuge

Of curtains; he stumbles down our short street
Thankfully passing us. I pause, wait,

Then to breathe relief lean on the sill
And for a second only my blood is still

With atavism. That rose he smashed frays
Ribboned across our hedge, recalling days

Of burned countryside, illicit braid:
A cause ruined before, a world betrayed.

Child of Our Time

for Aengus

Yesterday I knew no lullaby
But you have taught me overnight to order
This song, which takes from your final cry
Its tune, from your unreasoned end its reason,
Its rhythm from the discord of your murder
Its motive from the fact you cannot listen.

We who should have known how to instruct
With rhymes for your waking, rhythms for your sleep,
Names for the animals you took to bed,
Tales to distract, legends to protect,
Later an idiom for you to keep
And living, learn, must learn from you, dead,

To make our broken images rebuild
Themselves around your limbs, your broken
Image, find for your sake whose life our idle
Talk has cost, a new language. Child
Of our time, our times have robbed your cradle.
Sleep in a world your final sleep has woken.

17 May 1974

A Soldier's Son

for Andrew

A young man's war it is, a young man's war,
Or so they say and so they go to wage
This struggle where, armoured only in nightmare,
Every warrior is under age –
A son seeing each night leave, as father,
A man who may become the ancestor

In a backstreet stabbing, at a ghetto corner
Of future wars and further fratricide.
Son of a soldier who saw war on the ground,
Now cross the peace lines I have made for you
To find on this side if not peace then honour,
Your heritage, knowing as I do

That in the cross-hairs of his gun he found
You his only son, and when he aimed
And when the bullet cracked, the only sound
Was of his son rifling his heart. You twist
That heart today; you are his killed, his maimed.
He is your war; you are his pacifist.

The Famine Road

'Idle as trout in light Colonel Jones,
these Irish, give them no coins at all; their bones
need toil, their characters no less.' Trevelyan's
seal blooded the deal table. The Relief
Committee deliberated: 'Might it be safe,
Colonel, to give them roads, roads to force
from nowhere, going nowhere of course?'

> *'one out of every ten and then*
> *another third of those again*
> *women – in a case like yours.'*

Sick, directionless they worked; fork, stick
were iron years away; after all could
they not blood their knuckles on rock, suck
April hailstones for water and for food?
Why for that, cunning as housewives, each eyed –
as if at a corner butcher – the other's buttock.

> *'anything may have caused it, spores,*
> *a childhood accident; one sees*
> *day after day these mysteries.'*

Dusk: they will work tomorrow without him.
They know it and walk clear; he has become
a typhoid pariah, his blood tainted, although
he shares it with some there. No more than snow
attends its own flakes where they settle
and melt, will they pray by his death rattle.

> *'You never will, never you know*
> *but take it well woman, grow*
> *your garden, keep house, good-bye.'*

'It has gone better than we expected, Lord
Trevelyan, sedition, idleness, cured
in one; from parish to parish, field to field,
the wretches work till they are quite worn,
then fester by their work; we march the corn
to the ships in peace; this Tuesday I saw bones
out of my carriage window, your servant Jones.'

> *'Barren, never to know the load*
> *of his child in you, what is your body*
> *now if not a famine road ?'*

Cyclist with Cut Branches

Country hands on the handlebars,
A bicycle bisecting cars
   Lethal and casual
In rush hour traffic, I remember
Seeing, as I watched that September
   For you as usual.

Like rapid mercury abused
By summer heat where it is housed
   In slender telling glass,
My heart taking grief's temperature,
That summer, lost its powers to cure,
   Its gift to analyse.

Jasmine and the hyacinth,
The lintel mortar and the plinth
    Of spring across his bars,
Like globed grapes at first I thought,
Then at last more surely wrought
    Like winter's single stars,

Until I glimpsed not him but you
Like an animal the packs pursue
    To covert in a forest,
And knew the branches were not spring's
Nor ever summer's ample things,
    But decay's simple trust.

And since we had been like them cut
But from the flowering not the root
    Then we had thanks to give –
That they and we had opened once,
Had found the light, had lost its glance
    And still had lives to live.

Song

Where in blind files
Bats outsleep the frost
Water slips through stones
Too fast, too fast
For ice; afraid he'd slip
By me I asked him first.

Round as a bracelet
Clasping the wet grass,
An adder drowsed by berries
Which change blood to cess.
Dreading delay's venom
I risked the first kiss.

My skirt in my hand,
Lifting the hem high
I forded the river there.
Drops splashed my thigh.
Ahead of me at last
He turned at my cry:

'Look how the water comes
Boldly to my side;
See the waves attempt
What you have never tried.'
He late that night
Followed the leaping tide.

The Botanic Gardens

for Kevin

Guided by love, leaving aside dispute –
Guns on the pages of newspapers, the sound
Urgent of peace – we drive in real pursuit
Of another season, spring, where each has found
Something before, new, and then sense
In the Botanic Gardens, terms of reference.

You take my hand. Three years ago, your bride,
I felt your heart in darkness, a full moon
Hauling mine to it like a tide.
Still at night our selves reach to join,
To twine like these trees in peace and stress,
Before the peril of unconsciousness.

Corsican pine, guerilla poison plants –
The first gardener here by foreign carriage
And careful seeding in this circumference
Imitated the hours of our marriage:
The flowers of forced proximity, swollen, fed,
Flourishing here, usually sheltered,

Exposed this once. Now you have overstepped
My reach, searching for something this February
Like a scholar in poor light over a script,
Able at last to decipher its coded story
And so preoccupied you do not see
My absence in the conservatory

Where you, while African grotesqueries
Sweat in sandy heat, at last stand
Wondering at cacti, deformed trees
Most ridicule. Each pumpkin history
Turns coach at a touch of your hand.
I watch and love you in your mystery.

Prisoners

I saw him first lost in the lion cages
Of the zoo; before he could tear it out
I screamed my heart out; but his rages
Had been left behind. All he had left was his lope,
his mane, as bored as a socialite
With her morning post, I saw him slit
A rabbit open like an envelope.

Everything after that was parody –
I glimpsed him at the hearth in a jet
Cat, in a school annual tamed in type,
In a screen safari. The irony
Of finding him here in the one habitat
I never expected, alive and well in our suburban
World, present as I garden, sweep,

Wring the teacloth dry, domesticate
Acanthus in a bowl, orbit each chair
Exactly round our table. Your pullover
Lies on the bed upstairs, spread there where
You can no more free yourself from the bars
Of your arms round me than can over
Us the lion flee, silently, his stars.

Ready for Flight

From this I will not swerve nor fall nor falter:
If around your heart the crowds disperse,
And I who at their whim now freeze or swelter
Am allowed to come to a more temperate place,

And if a runner starts to run to me
Dispatched by you, crying that all is trampled
Underfoot, terraces smashed, the entry
Into holy places rudely sampled,

Then I would come at once my love with love
Bringing to wasted areas the sight
Of butterfly and swan and turtle dove
Their wings ruffled like sails ready for flight.

In such surroundings, after the decease
Of devils, you and I would live in peace.

Sisters

for Nessa my own

Now it is winter and the hare
Imitates the hillside snow,
Crouches in his frame of ice,
The dormouse in his wheel of fur,
While in caves hour by hour
The bat glistens in reverse.

Snowdrops poised for assassination
Broadcast, white in the face, the stress
Of first bursting out of a prison
Where winter grips the warder's keys
By day, then at the dusk's tilt
Loops them to Orion's belt.

In Monkstown bay a young seal
Surfaces, sleuth hound of herring;
Gulls shriek as he steals their meal
But I, getting the hint of spring
As a fisherman an Armada hull,
Welcome his unexpected skull.

For you, as his outline through
The spring tide comes to view,
Spring to mind. In such disguise
Our love survived as the sea with ease
Becomes with granite a graphic twin,
Tumbling like a harlequin.

At seven years, the age of reason,
The ready child communicates
With Christ, according to our church.
Seven years ago in the silly season
And for such reasons our two hearts
Were put outside each other's reach.

The fable goes, becoming warmer
Every second against his breast,
Christ's blood created the first informer,
The robin redbreast: and still the thirst
For knowledge and blood, they still remain,
And still we turn to still the pain.

For it was I, I who betrayed
By letters unwritten, unlifted phones,
Unspoken words and now would have
You and those seven years re-made,
That I exhume these sad bones,
I who wish them another grave.

No shoulders, not a 'soldier on',
No gunshots, nothing of that kind:
We both knew soldiers are unknown.
But since you hauled my one eye blind,
Round like the morning globe to meet
Light, could my thanks be discreet?

O and my sister, not a sound
Could bribe its way into this silence,
Nor ricochet where you have found
In one stunned heart, which must now trounce
Breaking, if not a breathing space,
Well then a sister's grim embrace.

And in your ear a final word:
That we remember all our pain
Has saved us from a final fate,
One worse than death, has left us scarred
But strangely safe for we remain
From these others separate:

The three harridans who toy
With human life, who in the cut
And thrust of gossip, never
Noticed one untwisted joy,
One sisterhood, so could not sever
Ours with an idle, chill gesture.

The Laws of Love

for Mary Robinson

At first light the legislator
Who schooled you, creator
Of each force, each element,
Its secret law, its small print
Nature – while dawn, baptismal as waters
Which broke early in dark, began –
First saw the first of your daughters
Become in your arms a citizen.

How easy for you to have made
For her a perfumed stockade,
How easy for you to impose
Laws and structures, torts for those
Fragments which matter less and less
As all fragments, and we must bless
The child, its murderer, defend
This chaos somehow which must end

With order. But who can separate
Hatred from its opposite
Or judge which is the other's source
Today, unless perhaps that force
Which makes your Moy in its ridge pool
Prime teenage trout for butchery,
While at the same time fulfil
The blood-tie of the tide, as we

Once new found sisters, each grown miser
With new found blood began to trade
Salmond for Shakespeare, none the wiser
Then but now I see it focus
Slowly a miracle, a closing wound.
That sisters kill, that sisters die, must mock us
Now, unless, with separate speech we find
For them new blood, for them now plead

Another world for whose horizons,
For whose anguish no reprieve
Exists unless new citizens,
And, as we found, laws of love –
We two whose very first worlds fell
Like wishes down a wishing well,
Ungranted, had we known, unwanted
Yet still there as the well is, haunted.

The Family Tree

I miss them as though they had existed:
My aunt, her port wine cheeks and at her apron
Keys singing, keys to the port, the round
Steak, dry biscuits, mutton, twisted
Crochet – whistle clean – and for her son,
Her only son, bridal linen. I have found

Them most unexpectedly, here
In this wood growing as trees: here
Closely grouped in one arrested sphere
Stand my uncles, unable even once
To shed their gravity, just as the dense
Yew, solemn in January is drear

Still in April, still cloaked in the same
Serious loop and swag of dark branches
Which will not lose a leaf for spring or autumn,
But mine their gravity, mine their hunches
On the market, their presence at the races,
Mine their stance, mine their stolid faces,

Their girths broad as trunks. Look,
On the right my cousins, lace at the wrists,
Ruffles at the throat, clustered as
Laburnums, flinging out their delicate
Inviting blooms in hollow courtesy
Which this spring till they disintegrate –

All empty beckoning, yellow malice –
Will wage their sterile fight, their arid battle
Pleasuring to poison enemy cattle,
Innocent children now. I lose my solace
In them, now my vision blurs, I see
Only woods lost in my family tree.

Naoise at Four

The trap baited for them snaps.
Like forest pests they fall for it,
Like humans writhe, like both submit.
Three brothers die, their three saps
Spill until their split kith
Heals into an Irish myth.

Naoise, named for one of these,
You stand in our kitchen, sip
Milk from a mottled cup
From our cupboard. Our unease
Vanishes with one smile
As each suburban, modern detail

Distances us from old lives
Old deaths, but nightly on our screen
New ones are lost, wounds open,
And I despair of what perspective
On this sudden Irish fury
Will solve it to a folk memory.

Godson, little creditor,
Your spiritual good in trust
To me demands at very least
I be your spirit's auditor
Until the moment you first try
To make your own inventory.

Your father gossips of the wood
Around your house, a lucky context
Where values can be learned, fixed,
A truce with life negotiated
On terms you yourself can make
Unlike your luckless namesake.

You drain your cup; your love
Is a closed circuit like your glove
In your mother's. There is nothing to sell you
Here, invest in nothing: at home
Badgers, voles enrich your time:
Your currency will not devalue.

Anon

I sympathise but wonder what he fled
From: the press, an unimpressed boss,
His wife smirking as he came to bed,
Aunts whispering that he'd turned to verse
As though to vice?
       Maybe they weren't far wrong.
Some guilty midnight, the idea spawned, shawled
In words, he abandoned it, a foundling
To be forever afterwards the love child
Of anthologies. Then back to work,
His moment's indiscretion a secret
Until one day rifling through a book
To find it, accusing, illegitimate.

From the Irish of Pangur Ban

for Mairin

Myself and Pangur, cat and sage
Go each about our business;
I harass my beloved page,
He his mouse.

Fame comes second to the peace
Of study, a still day.
Unenvying, Pangur's choice
Is child's play.

Neither bored, both hone
At home a separate skill,
Moving after hours alone
To the kill.

When at last his net wraps,
After a sly fight,
Around a mouse, mine traps
Sudden insight.

On my cell wall here,
His sight fixes, burning,
Searching; my old eyes peer
At new learning,

And his delight when his claws
close on his prey
Equals mine when sudden clues
Light my way.

So we find by degrees
Peace in solitude,
Both of us, solitaries,
Have each the trade

We love: Pangur, never idle
Day or night
Hunts mice; I hunt each riddle
From dark to light.

Elegy for a Youth Changed to a Swan

from Lir, the Irish legend

Now the March woods will miss his step,
Finding out a way at spring's start
To break at once their bracken and their sleep,
And now have lost, robbed of their rightful part,
Some hawk a master's hand, some maid a heart.

Urchins of the hurdled hawthorn, sparrows,
Spiders webbed in hedges, brown
Field mice, wheeled, sleeping in their furrows,
Spared by the plough, stout with corn –
These were familiars of Lir's son

No less than the stiff, aloof lily,
The oak and the hawk, the Moy salmon
On February mornings, unruly
With new life and the flushed rowan
Stooped with berries, October's paragon.

O sap of the green forest like a sea
Rise in the sycamore and rowan,
Rise in the wild plum and chestnut tree
Until the woods become a broad ocean
For my son in his wilderness, my swan,

That he may see breaking on his breast
And wings not the waters of his exile,
Nor the pawn of the wind, the cold crest,
But branches of the white beam and the maple,
Boughs of the almond and the laurel.

O Fons Bandusiae

Horace 3: XIII

Bold as crystal, bright as glass,
Your waters leap while we appear
Carrying to your woodland shrine
Gifts below your worthiness:
Grape and flower, Bandusia,
Yellow hawksbeard, ready wine.

And tomorrow we will bring
A struggling kid, his temples sore
With early horns, as sacrifice.
Tomorrow his new trumpeting
Will come to nothing, when his gore
Stains and thaws your bright ice.

Canicula, the lamp of drought,
The summer's fire, leaves your grace
Inviolate in the woods where
Everyday you spring to comfort
The broad bull in his trace,
The herd out of the shepherd's care.

With every fountain, every spring
Of legend, I will set you down
In praise and immortal spate:
These waters which drop gossiping
To ground, this wet surrounding stone
And this green oak I celebrate.

Dependence Day

for Fran McCracken

Snail, churl of dawn and dark,
Day is christened in your laces.
Your industry puts out of work
The peacock's airs, the python's graces.

Since, worm, your mulberry, your cocoon
Has nourished you to nourish silk,
How often have you been forgotten
When skirts came pouring down like milk?

Shadow thrown away like dirt
Between the morning and the night
How necessary was your hurt?
Now, now instruct me Christ

So my heart might not harden
Since yours at last found light relief:
Sleeping partners in the garden,
Your final acolyte a thief.

Conversation with an Inspector of Taxes

after Mayakovsky

No, Comrade Inspector, I won't sit down,
Thank you; forgive me taxing your time.
What a delicate matter this business of mine
Is, the more difficult since I am
Concerned to discern the role of the poet
Within the ranks of the proletariat.

If you knew how you've added to my troubles
Taxing me like a shopkeeper or kulak –
For six months you claim five hundred roubles
And twenty-five for the forms I didn't send back.
Yet I work the same as any, look what I've lost
In production and what my materials cost.

Perhaps I should explain it in your idiom:
What you call a promissory note
Is roughly the equivalent of rhyme
To us, owed to each and every alternate
Line while in the petty cash of sense
We moisten the coins of nuance.

Suppose I select a word to go
Into a line, it won't fit, I start
To force it and the next thing I know
The seams of the stanza strain apart.
Comrade Inspector, I can give
Assurance that words come expensive.

To revert now to poetic licence:
Metaphorically speaking my rhyming
Is a keg of dynamite, my lines
Smoulder towards it slowly, the timing
Device detonates and finally
The whole poem blows sky high.

Accusing me from your questionnaire
I see, 'Have you travelled in the course
Of business?' What if every year
I've bitted and stampeded Pegasus
Till both of us were worn? Have some sense.
Take into account the following instance.

There may be in Venezuela five
Or six pristine rhymes undiscovered.
If in pursuit of them I have
Tax to pay on travel, then my fevered
Search would draw too mean a loan
For poetry to sack the unknown.

Considering all this will you allow
Me a small mercenary reprieve?
I'll accept an inch of clay, a plough;
I'll be a peasant. Otherwise I achieve
So little by this speech that its effect,
Nil on you, on me I expect,

Will be years from now, I am sure,
These lines like ones in a puppet show,
Will jerk you back, inking your signature
On final demands and so, Comrade, so
I will have guaranteed your encore
Years after I have died and lie a pauper,

Crushed not by you bureaucrat
Though your claims are irritating, true,
But by the vast claims on a poet
I could not meet. All my debts to you
Are those of any chance financial sinner
But those to follow are my debts of honour:

To the Red Army, boiling across frontiers
In a wash of Cossack stallions, coats
Threaded from goat hide, unshaved hairs
Masking them like bandits, their supporters
Cheering them as the musket shots
Ventilate each of their deserters:

To the winter flowering cherry of Japan,
Frail as a foundling which never found
In my verse even the shelter given
To it by the snows which surround
Its blossom stealthily like rags heaped
Over a sprawled vagrant where he slept:

Finally I know myself indebted
Beyond anything I can return
To the fastness of my winter cradle,
Because somehow I never celebrated
Its bleak skies; to this day they remain
Unsung while my tongue is idle.

The Atlantic Ocean

after Mayakovsky

This stone, this Spanish stone, flings light
Like acid in my eyes; walls splice the day.
Our freighter chokes, then belches anthracite.
Fresh water up by noon; we are away.
    A shrivelled Europe faces
    Starboard; our guzzling boat
    Bloats on fish, swallows, chases
    The anchor down its throat.

Waves are conjurors, splashes sleeves,
Up which aces of past and future hide.
One man finds love, another what he grieves
By watching; to me they are another side
    Of life, not one to do
    With retrospect or manners
    But with the ballyhoo
    Of war, the hoist of banners.

Out of this ocean now, its menacing storms,
Out of its cryptic structures, its tribal
Tides, out of its secret order, from the cabal
Of trade wind and water, look, a Soviet forms
    A squad of drops batters
    The sky for a second, wears
    Out its force, then turns and tears
    Each imperial crest to tatters.

The waves are agitating now, the sea
Itself becomes the theatre of the battle:
Lesser waves congregate, they settle
On a policy for all and all agree
    Not to abandon their will
    To fight, their fierce airs
    Their stormy posture until
    Victory is theirs:

So what has started well can flourish still,
As for example underneath the tide
The marvel of structured self-perfecting coral
Now a milestone, soon to be a guide
    To the she-whale, the sperm-whale nosing
    Clear of the shark, the porpoises
    Braceleting the ships' bows,
    The octopus intricately dozing.

No wonder it beats like an alternate heart in me,
No wonder its drops fill and fall from my eyes
In familiar drops; it's in the family.
At last I see, at last I recognise
    In its wild station,
    Its ice and riot, its other
    Prowess, of my revolution
    The elder brother.

Chorus of the Shadows

after Nelly Sachs

Puppets we are, strung by a puppet master.
He knows the theatre of the absurd, he understands
Murder too well, outrage, grief, disaster.
He puts the show on in hell. By his permission
We are moths fired and turned on his obsession,
And his hands,

Are pinned to the dust, darken the hangman's threats
Give depth to the noose and our dimensions greet him,
The victim, as he plummets. No wonder we are
Weary of our own silhouettes.
Now we are driven to it, now we deliver
An ultimatum

To the planet which scripts our part. Take away
Light and we will not undertake love
Any longer. Give us a new part to play
In the day of a child or a stake in the luck, the frail
Perfect luck of a dragonfly above
The rim of a well.

The Greek Experience

Until that night, the night I lost my wonder,
He was my deity, first of my mentors,
  Master craftsman; mere apprentice
  I, hearing how Croesus, to entice
    The priestess predators
Wooed a false oracle. But mine the truth
I thought, marvelling at Cyrus tuned to plunder
By oboes, playing on Persia. But who cares now?
My name means nothing here, his, Herodotus

Towers in Babylon, salts the Aegean
Is silted into each Ionic ear.
> Only I know the charlatan,
> The mountebank who tongued
> > Day slyly to night
To suit his purpose. Prepared to be harangued
And angled by his anecdotes, his school
Of stories, instead I found that night
A mind incapable of insight as a mule

Of generation. 'The times need iron men,
Pragmatists,' he said, 'who can devise
> For those problems which arise
> So frequently a swift solution.
> > A man such as this:
He is a soldier, able to lead, to train.
His stallion where the Gyndes finds the Tigris
And those two rivers join in dissolution
In the Gulf, drowned; the waters combed its mane.

'Now he was leading Persian against Mede
But called a truce, cut his troops in two
> And swore revenge on the water.
> He was the first to take his blade,
> > The first to teach the lesson
With stabs and thrusts. He prolonged the slaughter
All summer. The river now is channelled.
Those are the men we need.' I listened, chilled.
'A soldier is lost to us; now a deadly assassin.

'Lies in wait for us all' was my recourse.
'Nonsense,' he said; but I was trying to live
> The ambush, the sudden fever
> The assault of a single force,
> > An instant, the divider
Of a man from his own mind, his mythic source,
His origin in animal and primitive,
Which changes centaur into horse and rider,
The sort of wound a man might imitate forever.

And seeing hacked limbs, I was their screams,
Their first vomit of terror, but I was his dreams
 Also as, victim to his victim,
 He saw himself split again
  And turned away alone,
Forever puzzled. 'He will kill again of course,'
I said. He smiled, slurred, 'I am
The traveller after all; you can't have known
The hardship now in getting a good horse.'

Suburban Woman

I

Town and country at each other's throat –
between a space of truce until one night

walls began to multiply, to spawn
like lewd whispers of the goings-on,

the romperings, the rape on either side,
the smiling killing, that you were better dead

than let them get you. But they came, armed
with blades and ladders, with slimed

knives, day after day, week by week –
a proxy violation. She woke

one morning to the usual story: withdrawing,
neither side had gained, but there, dying,

caught in cross-fire, her past lay, bleeding
from wounds each meant for each, which needing

each other for other wars they could not inflict
one on another. Haemorrhaging to hacked

roads, in back gardens, like a pride
of lions toiled for booty, tribal acres died

and her world with them. She saw their power to sever
with a scar. She is the sole survivor.

II

Morning: mistress of talcums, spun
and second cottons, run tights
she is, courtesan to the lethal
rapine of routine. The room invites.
She reaches to fluoresce the dawn.
The kitchen lights like a brothel.

III

The chairs dusted and the morning
coffee break behind, she starts pawning

her day again to the curtains, the red
carpets, the stair rods, at last to the bed,

the unmade bed where once in an underworld
of limbs, her eyes freckling the night like jewelled

lights on a cave wall, she, crying, stilled,
bargained out of nothingness her child,

bartered from the dark her only daughter.
Waking, her cheeks dried, to a brighter

dawn she sensed in her as in April earth
a seed, a life ransoming her death.

IV

Late, quiet across her garden
sunlight shifts like a cat
burglar, thieving perspectives,
leaving her in the last light
alone, where, as shadows harden,
lengthen, silent she perceives
veteran dead-nettles, knapweed
crutched on walls, a summer's seed
of roses trenched in ramsons, and stares
at her life falling with her flowers,
like military tribute or the tears
of shell-shocked men, into arrears.

V

Her kitchen blind down – a white flag –
the day's assault over, now she will shrug

a hundred small surrenders off as images
still born, unwritten metaphors, blank pages

and on this territory, blindfold, we meet
at last, veterans of a defeat

no truce will heal, no formula prevent
breaking out fresh again; again the print

of twigs stalking her pillow will begin
a new day and all her victims then –

hopes unreprieved, hours taken hostage –
will newly wake, while I, on a new page

will watch, like town and country, word, thought
look for ascendancy, poise, retreat

leaving each line maimed, my forces used.
Defeated we survive, we two, housed

together in my compromise, my craft
who are of one another the first draft.

Ode to Suburbia

Six o'clock: the kitchen bulbs which blister
Your dark, your housewives starting to nose
Out each other's day, the claustrophobia
Of your back gardens varicose
With shrubs make an ugly sister
Of you suburbia.

How long ago did the glass in your windows subtly
Silver into mirrors which again
And again show the same woman
Shriek at a child, which multiply
A dish, a brush, ash,
The gape of a fish

In the kitchen, the gape of a child in the cot?
You swelled so that when you tried
The silver slipper on your foot
It pinched your instep and the common
Hurt which touched you made
You human.

No creatures of your streets will feel the touch
Of a wand turning the wet sinews
Of fruit suddenly to a coach,
While this rat without leather reins
Or a whip or britches continues
Sliming your drains.

No magic here. Yet you encroach until
The shy countryside, fooled
By your plainness falls, then rises
From your bed changed, schooled
Forever by your skill,
Your compromises.

Midnight and your metamorphosis
Is now complete, although the mind
Which spinstered you might still miss
Your mystery now, might still fail
To see your powers defined
By this detail:

By this creature drowsing now in every house,
The same lion who tore stripes
Once off zebras, who now sleeps
Small beside the coals and may
On a red letter day
Catch a mouse.

The Hanging Judge

Come to the country where justice is seen to be done,
Done daily. Come to the country where
Sentence is passed by word of mouth and raw
Boys split like infinitives. Look, here
We hanged our son, our only son
And hang him still and still we call it law.

James Lynch Fitzstephen, magistrate,
First Citizen of Galway, 1493,
Spanish merchant trader, his horror
Of deceit a by-word, a pillar of society
With one weakness, Walter, whose every trait
Reversed his like a signature in a mirror.

The torches splutter, the dancing, supple,
Spanish-taught, starts. James Lynch Fitzstephen
May disapprove but he, a man of principle
Recalls young Gomez is a guest in town,
And the girl beside, his son's choice, may restore
A new name and honour in an heir.

Dawn: Gomez dead, in a wood: the Spanish heart
Which softened to her rigid with the steel
Of Walter Lynch's blade. Wild justice there –
Now to its restraint, but not repeal,
He returns, friendless, to be met
By his father, mounted, hunting. In the stare

Which passed slowly between them, a history
Poises: repression and rebellion, the scaffold
And its songs, the principle unsung
Are clues in this judicial murder to a mystery
Unsolved still and only to be told
As a ghost story against a haunting, –

As you, father, haunt me: the rope trails
From your fingers, below you the abyss.
Your arms balanced as the scales of justice,
You loop him while from your eyes fall other scales
Too late, tears of doubt, tears of remorse
Dropping on your own neck like a noose.

IN HER OWN IMAGE
1980

Tirade for the Mimic Muse

I've caught you out. You slut. You fat trout.
So here you are fumed in candle-stink.
Its yellow balm exhumes you for the glass.
How you arch and pout in it!
How you poach your face in it!
Anyone would think you were a whore –
An ageing out-of-work kind-hearted tart.
I know you for the ruthless bitch you are:
Our criminal, our tricoteuse, our Muse –
Our Muse of Mimic Art.

Eye-shadow, swivel brushes, blushers,
Hot pinks, rouge pots, sticks,
Ice for the pores, a mud mask –
All the latest tricks.
Not one of them disguise
That there's a dead millennium in your eyes.
You try to lamp the sockets of your loss:
The lives that famished for your look of love.
Your time is up. There's not a stroke, a flick
Can make your crime cosmetic.

With what drums and dances, what deceits
Rituals and flatteries of war,
Chants and pipes and witless empty rites
And war-like men
And wet-eyed patient women
You did protect yourself from horrors,
From the lizarding of eyelids
From the whiskering of nipples,
From the slow betrayals of our bedroom mirrors –
How you fled

The kitchen screw and the rack of labour,
The wash thumbed and the dish cracked,
The scream of beaten women,
The crime of babies battered,
The hubbub and the shriek of daily grief
That seeks asylum behind suburb walls –
A world you could have sheltered in your skirts –
And well I know and how I see it now,
The way you latched your belt and itched your hem
And shook it off like dirt.

And I who mazed my way to womanhood
Through all your halls of mirrors, making faces,
To think I waited on your trashy whim!
Hoping your lamp and flash,
Your glass, might show
This world I needed nothing else to know
But love and again love and again love.
In a nappy stink, by a soaking wash
Among stacked dishes
Your glass cracked,

Your luck ran out. Look. My words leap
Among your pinks, your stench pots and sticks.
They scatter shadow, swivel brushes, blushers.
Make your face naked.
Strip your mind naked.
Drench your skin in a woman's tears.
I will wake you from your sluttish sleep.
I will show you true reflections, terrors.
You are the Muse of all our mirrors.
Look in them and weep.

In Her Own Image

It is her eyes:
the irises are gold
and round they go
like the ring on my wedding finger,
round and round

and I can't touch
their histories or tears.
To think they were once my satellites!
They shut me out now.
Such light years!

She is not myself
anymore she is not
even in my sky
anymore and I
am not myself.

I will not disfigure
her pretty face.
Let her wear amethyst thumbprints,
a family heirloom,
a sort of burial necklace

and I know just the place:
Where the wall glooms,
where the lettuce seeds,
where the jasmine springs
no surprises

I will bed her.
She will bloom there,
second nature to me,
the one perfection
among compromises.

In His Own Image

I was not myself, myself.
The celery feathers,
the bacon flitch,
the cups deep on the shelf
and my cheek
coppered and shone
in the kettle's paunch,
my mouth
blubbed in the tin of the pan –
they were all I had to go on.

How could I go on
With such meagre proofs of myself?
I woke day after day.
Day after day I was gone.
From the self I was last night.

And then he came home tight.

Such a simple definition!
How did I miss it?
Now I see
that all I needed
was a hand
to mould my mouth
to scald my cheek,
was this concussion
by whose lights I find
my self-possession,
where I grow complete.

He splits my lip with his fist,
shadows my eye with a blow,
knuckles my neck to its proper angle.
What a perfectionist!
His are a sculptor's hands:
they summon
form from the void,
they bring

me to myself again.
I am a new woman.

Anorexic

Flesh is heretic.
My body is a witch.
I am burning it.

Yes I am torching
her curves and paps and wiles.
They scorch in my self denials.

How she meshed my head
in the half-truths
of her fevers

till I renounced
milk and honey
and the taste of lunch.

I vomited
her hungers.
Now the bitch is burning.

I am starved and curveless.
I am skin and bone.
She has learned her lesson.

Thin as a rib
I turn in sleep.
My dreams probe

a claustrophobia
a sensuous enclosure.
How warm it was and wide

once by a warm drum,
once by the song of his breath
and in his sleeping side.

Only a little more,
only a few more days
sinless, foodless.

I will slip
back into him again
as if I have never been away.

Caged so
I will grow
angular and holy

past pain
keeping his heart
such company

as will make me forget
in a small space
the fall

into forked dark,
into python needs
heaving to hips and breasts
and lips and heat
and sweat and fat and greed.

Mastectomy

My ears heard
their words.
I didn't believe them.

No, even through my tears
they couldn't deceive me.
Even so

I could see
through them
to the years

opening
their arteries,
fields gulching

into trenches
cuirasses stenching,
a mulch of heads

and towns
as prone
to bladed men

as women.
How well
I recognised

the specialist
freshing death
across his desk,

the surgeon,
blade-handed,
standing there

urging patience.
How well
they have succeeded!

I have stopped bleeding
I look down.
It has gone.

So they have taken off
what slaked them first
what they have hated since:

blue-veined
white-domed
home

of wonder
and the wetness
of their dreams.

I flatten
to their looting,
to the sleight

of their plunder.
I am a brute site.
Theirs is the true booty.

Solitary

Night:
An oratory of dark,
a chapel of unreason.

Here in the shrubbery
the shrine.
I am its votary,
its season.

Flames
single
to my fingers

expert
to pick out
their heart,
the sacred heat

none may violate.
You could die for this.
The gods could make you blind.

I defy them.
I know,
only I know

these incendiary
and frenzied ways:
I am alone

no one's here,
no one sees
my hands

fan and cup,
my thumbs tinder.
How it leaps

from spark to blaze!
I flush.
I darken.

How my flesh summers,
how my mind shadows,
meshed in this brightness

how my cry
blasphemes
light and dark,
screams
land from sea,
makes word flesh
that now makes me

animal
inanimate, satiate,

and back I go
to a slack tip,
a light.

I stint my worship,
the cold watch I keep.
Fires flint somewhere else.
I winter
into sleep.

Menses

It is dark again.

I am sick of it
filled with it,
dulled by it,
thick with it.

To be the mere pollution of her wake!
a water cauled by her light,
a slick haul,
a fallen self,
a violence,
a daughter.

I am the moon's looking glass.
My days are moon-dials.
She will never be done with me.
She needs me.
She is dry.

I leash to her,
a sea,
a washy heave,
a tide.
Only my mind is free

among the ruffian growths,
the bindweed
and the meadowsweet,
the riff-raff of my garden.

How I envy them;
each filament,
each anther bred
from its own style,
its stamen,
is to itself a christening,
is to itself a marriage bed.

They fall to earth,
so ignorant
so innocent
of the sweated waters
and the watered salts,
of ecstasy,
of birth.

They are street-walkers,
lesbians,
nuns.
I am not one of them

and how they'd pity me

now as dusk encroaches
and she comes

looking for her looking-glass.
And it is me.

Yes it is me
she poaches her old face in.
I am bloated with her waters.
I am barren with her blood.
Another hour
and she will addle me

till I begin
to think like her.
As when I've grown
round and obscene with child.
Or when I moan,
for him between the sheets,
then I begin to know
that I am bright and original
and that my light's my own.

Witching

My gifts
are nightly,
shifty, bookish.

By my craft
I bald the grass,
abort the birth

of calves
and warts.
I study dark.

Another age
and I'd have been
waisted

in a hedgy rage
of prejudice
and hate.

But times have changed.
They will be brought
to book.

these my enemies –
and bell
and candle too –

who breed
and breed,
who talk and talk –

birth
and bleeding
the bacteria of feeds.

Midnight.
Now I own
the earth.

The witching hour.
You'd think
you'd think

the bitches
couldn't reach
me here.

But here they are.
The nursery lights
they shine, they shine,

they multiply
they douse
mine!

But I
know
what to do:

I will
reverse
their arson,

make
a pyre of my haunch

and so
the last thing
they know

will be
the stench
of my crotch.

Flaming
tindering
I'll singe

a page
of history
for these my sisters

for those kin
they kindled.
Yes it's my turn

to stack
the twigs
and twig the fire

and smell
how well

a woman's
flesh
can burn.

Exhibitionist

I wake to dark,
a window slime of dew.
Time to start

working
from the text,
making

from this trash
and gimmickry
of sex

my aesthetic:
a hip first,
a breast,

a slow
shadow strip
out of clothes

that bushelled me
asleep.
What an artist am I!

Barely light
and yet –
cold shouldering

clipped laurel,
nippling the road –
I subvert

sculpture,
the old mode;
I skin

I dimple clay,
I flesh,
I rump stone.

This is my way –
to strip and strip
until

my dusk flush
nude shade,
hush

of hip,
back bone,
thigh

blacks light
and I
become the night.

What stars
I harvest
to my dark!

Cast down
Lucifers,
spruce

businessmen,
their eyes
cast down.

I have them now.
I'll teach them now.
I'll show them how

in offices,
their minds
blind on files,

the view
blues through
my curves and arcs.

They are
a part
of my dark plan:

Into the gutter
of their lusts
I burn

the shine
of my flesh.
Let them know

for a change
the hate
and discipline,

the lusts
that prison
and the light that is

unyielding
frigid
constellate.

Making Up

My naked face;
I wake to it.
How it's dulsed and shrouded!
It's a cloud,

a dull pre–dawn.
But I'll soon
see to that.
I push the blusher up,

I raddle
and I prink,
pinking bone
till my eyes

are
a rouge–washed
flush on water.
Now the base

pales and wastes.
Light thins
from ear to chin,
whitening in

the ocean shine
mirror set
of my eyes
that I fledge

in old darks.
I grease and full
my mouth.
It won't stay shut:

I look
in the glass.
My face is made,
it says:

Take nothing, nothing
at its face value:
Legendary seas,
nakedness,

that up and stuck
lassitude
of thigh and buttock
that they prayed to –

it's a trick.
Myths
are made by men.
The truth of this

wave-raiding
sea-heaving
made-up
tale

of a face
from the source
of the morning
is my own:

Mine are the rouge pots,
the hot pinks,
the fledged
and edgy mix
of light and water
out of which
I dawn.

NIGHT FEED
1980

Domestic Interior

for Kevin

The woman is as round
as the new ring
ambering her finger.
The mirror weds her.
She has long since been bedded.

There is
about it all
a quiet search for attention,
like the unexpected shine
of a despised utensil.

The oils,
the varnishes,
the cracked light,
the worm of permanence –
all of them supplied by Van Eyck –

by whose edict she will stay
burnished, fertile,
on her wedding day,
interred in her joy.
Love, turn.

The convex of your eye
that is so loving, bright
and constant yet shows
only this woman in her varnishes,
who won't improve in the light.

But there's a way of life
that is its own witness:
Put the kettle on, shut the blind.
Home is a sleeping child,
an open mind

and our effects,
shrugged and settled
in the sort of light
jugs and kettles
grow important by.

Night Feed

This is dawn.
Believe me
This is your season, little daughter.
The moment daisies open,
The hour mercurial rainwater
Makes a mirror for sparrows.
It's time we drowned our sorrows.

I tiptoe in.
I lift you up
Wriggling
In your rosy, zipped sleeper.
Yes, this is the hour
For the early bird and me
When finder is keeper.

I crook the bottle.
How you suckle!
This is the best I can be,
Housewife
To this nursery
Where you hold on,
Dear life.

A silt of milk.
The last suck.
And now your eyes are open,
Birth-coloured and offended.
Earth wakes.
You go back to sleep.
The feed is ended.

Worms turn.
Stars go in.
Even the moon is losing face.
Poplars stilt for dawn
And we begin
The long fall from grace.
I tuck you in.

Before Spring

They're done:
the seedlings
have leaves.
They'll be ready soon,

to put out
and harden off.
The art
is in the picking up –

not to touch
the spindly stems –
then mulching them
in terracotta pots

and finding
sunny beds
once the frosts
are over.

Then it's over –
the pride,
however slight,
in giving life.

That hard-blowing
wind outside
has a sound
of spring.

It won't be long.
No, it won't be long.
There is a melancholy
in the undersong:

Sweet child
asleep in your cot,
little seed-head,
there is time yet.

Energies

This is my time:
the twilight closing in,
a hissing on the ring,
stove noises, kettle steam
and children's kisses.

But the energy of flowers!
Their faces are so white –
my garden daisies –
they are so tight-fisted,
such economies of light.

In the dusk they have made hay:
in a banked radiance,
in an acreage of brightness
they are misering the day
while mine delays away

in chores left to do:
the soup, the bath, the fire
then bed-time,
up the stairs –
and there, there

the buttery curls,
the light,
the bran-fur of the teddy bear,
the fist like a night-time daisy,
damp and tight.

Hymn

Four a.m.
December.
A lamb
would perish out there.

The cutlery glitter
of that sky
has nothing in it
I want to follow.

Here is the star
of my nativity:
a nursery lamp
in a suburb window

behind which
is boiled glass, a bottle
and a baby all
hisses like a kettle.

The light goes out.
The blackbird takes up his part.
I wake by habit.
I know it all by heart:

these candles
and the altar
and psaltery of dawn.

And in the dark
as we slept
the world
was made flesh.

Partings

By the mercy
of the nursery light,
on the nursery wall,

among bears,
rattles, rag dolls,
in their big shadows,

we are one more and
inseparable again.
Day begins.

The world lives down
the dark union
of its wonders.

Your fingers fist in mine.
Outside the window
winter earth

discovers its horizon
as I cradle mine –

and light finds us
with the other loves
dawn sunders
to define.

Endings

A child
shifts in a cot.
No matter what happens now
I'll never fill one again.

It's a night
white things ember in:
jasmine and the shine –
flowering, opaline –
of the apple trees.

If I lean
I can see
what it is the branches end in:

The leaf.
The reach.
The blossom.
The abandon.

Fruit on a Straight-Sided Tray

When the painter takes the straight-sided tray
and arranges late melons with grapes and lemons,
the true subject is the space between them:

in which repose the pleasure of these ovals
is seen to be an assembly of possibilities;
a deliberate collection of cross purposes.

Gross blues and purples. Yellow and the shadow of bloom.
The room smells of metal polish The afternoon sun
brings light but not heat and no distraction from

the study of absences, the science of relationships
in which the abstraction is made actual: such as
fruit on a straight-sided tray; a homely arrangement.

This is the geometry of the visible, physical tryst
between substances, disguising for awhile the equation
that kills: you are my child and between us are

spaces. Distances. Growing to infinities.

Lights

We sailed the long way home
on a coal-burning ship.
There were bracelets on our freighter
of porpoises and water.

When we came where icebergs
mark the stars of the Bear
I leaned over the stern.
I was an urban twelve.

This was the Arctic garden.
A hard, sharkless Eden
porched by the North
A snow-shrubbed orchard

with Aurora Borealis –
apple-green and icy –
behind an ice wall.
But I was a child of the Fall:

I loved the python waves –
their sinuous, tailing blaze –
coiled in polar water
shoaling towards the cold

occasions where the daughters
of myth sang for sailors
who lay with them and lie
now in phosphor graves.

I lie half-awake.
The last star is out
and my book is shut.
These August dawns

green the sky at four.
The child asleep beside me
stirs away in dreams.
I am three times twelve.

No more the Aurora,
its apple-icy brightness.
But if I raise the window
and lean I can see

now over the garden,
its ice-cap of shadow,
a nursery light rising,
a midnight sun dawning.

The day will be the same –
its cold illusory rays,
the afternoon's enclosure
and dusk's ambiguous gleams.

Doubt still sharks
the close suburban night.
And all the lights I love
leave me in the dark.

After a Childhood Away from Ireland

One summer
we slipped in at dawn
on plum-coloured water
in the sloppy quiet.

The engines
of the ship stopped.
There was an eerie
drawing near,

a noiseless coming head-on
of red roofs, walls,
dogs, barley stooks.
Then we were there.

Cobh.
Coming home.
I had heard of this:
the ground the emigrants

resistless, weeping
laid their cheeks to,
put their lips to kiss.
Love is also memory.

I only stared.
What I had lost
was not land
but the habit of land:

whether of growing out of
or settling back on,
or being
defined by.

I climb
to your nursery.
I stand listening
to the dissonances

of the summer's day ending.
I bend to kiss you.
Your cheeks
are brick pink.

Monotony

The stilled hub
and polar drab
of the suburb
closes in.

In the round
of the staircase
my arms sheafing nappies,
I grow in and down

to an old spiral,
a well of questions,
an oracle:
will it tell me

am I
at these altars,
warm shrines,
washing machines, dryers

with their incense
of men and infants.
priestess
or sacrifice?

My late tasks
wait like children:
milk bottles,
the milkman's note.

Cold air
clouds the rinsed,
milky glass,
blowing clear

with a hint
of winter constellations:
will I find
my answer where

Virgo reaps?
Her arms sheafing
the hemisphere,
hour after frigid hour,

her virgin stars,
her maidenhead
married to force
harry us

to wed our gleams
to brute routines:
solstices,
small families.

The Muse Mother

My window pearls wet.
The bare rowan tree
berries rain.

I can see
from where I stand
a woman hunkering –
her busy hand
worrying a child's face,

working a nappy liner
over his sticky loud
round of a mouth.

Her hand's a cloud
across his face
making light and rain,
smiles and a frown,
a smile again.

She jockeys him to her hip,
pockets the nappy liner,
collars rain on her nape
and moves away

but my mind stays fixed:

if I could only decline her –
lost noun
out of context,
stray figure of speech –
from this rainy street

again to her roots,
she might teach me
a new language:

to be a sibyl
able to sing the past
in pure syllables,
limning hymns sung
to belly wheat or a woman –

able to speak at last
my mother tongue.

A Ballad of Home

How we kissed
in our half-built house!
It was slightly timbered,
a bit bricked, on stilts

and we were newly married.
We drove out at dusk
and picked our way to safety
through flint and grit and brick.

Like water through a porthole,
the sky poured in.
We sat on one step
making estimations

and hugged until the watchman
called and cursed and swung
his waterproof torch
into our calculations.

Ten years on
you wouldn't find now
an inch of spare ground.
Children in their cots,

books, a cat, plants
strain the walls' patience
and the last ounce of space.
And still every night

it all seems so sound.
But love why wouldn't it?
This house is built on our embrace
and there are worse foundations.

Patchwork or the Poet's Craft

I have been thinking at random
on the universe
or rather, how nothing in the universe
is random –

(there's nothing like presumption late at night.)

My sumptuous
trash bag of colours –
Laura Ashley cottons –
waits to be cut
and stitched and patched

but there's a mechanical feel
about the handle
of my second-hand sewing machine,
with its flowers
and *Singer* painted orange on it.
And its iron wheel.

My back is to the dark.
Somewhere out there
are stars and bits of stars
and little bits of bits.
And swiftnesses and brightnesses and drift.

But is it craft or art?

I will be here
till midnight,
cross-legged in the dining-room,
logging triangles and diamonds,
cutting and aligning,
finding greens in pinks
and burgundies in whites
until I finish it.

There's no reason in it.

Only when it's laid
right across the floor,
sphere on square
and seam on seam,
in a good light –
a night-sky spread –
will it start to hit me.

These are not bits.
They are pieces.

And the pieces fit.

In the Garden

Let's go out now
before the morning
gets warm.
Get your bicycle,

your teddy bear –
the one that's penny-coloured
like your hair –
and come.

I want to show you
what
I don't exactly know.
We'll find out.

It's our turn
in this garden,
by this light,
among the snails

and daisies –
one so slow
and one so closed –
to learn

I could show you things:
how the poplar root
is pushing through,
how your apple tree is doing,

how daisies
shut like traps.
But you're happy
as it is

and innocence
that until this
was just
an abstract water,

welling elsewhere
to refresh,
is risen here
my daughter:

Before the dew,
before the bloom
the snail was here.
The whole morning is his loom

and this is truth,
this is brute grace
as only instinct knows
how to live it

turn to me
your little face.
It shows a trace still,
an inkling of it.

Degas's Laundresses

You rise, you dawn
roll-sleeved Aphrodites,
out of a camisole brine,
a linen pit of stiches,
silking the fitted sheets
away from you like waves.

You seam dreams in the folds
of wash from which freshes
the whiff and reach of fields
where it bleached and stiffened.
Your chat's sabbatical:
brides, wedding outfits,

a pleasure of leisured women
are sweated into the folds,
the neat heaps of linen.
Now the drag of the clasp.
Your wrists basket your waist.
You round to the square weight.

Wait. There behind you.
A man. There behind you.
Whatever you do don't turn.
Why is he watching you?
Whatever you do don't turn.
Whatever you do don't turn.

See he takes his ease
staking his easel so,
slowly sharpening charcoal,
closing his eyes just so,
slowly smiling as if
so slowly he is

unbandaging his mind.
Surely a good laundress
would understand its twists.
its white turns,
its blind designs –

it's your winding sheet.

Woman in Kitchen

Breakfast over, islanded by noise,
she watches the machines go fast and slow.
She stands among them as they shake the house.
They move. Their destination is specific.
She has nowhere definite to go:
she might be a pedestrian in traffic.

White surfaces retract. White
sideboards light the white of walls.
Cups wink white in their saucers.
The light of day bleaches as it falls
on cups and sideboards. She could use
the room to tap with if she lost her sight.

Machines jigsaw everything she knows.
And she is everywhere among their furor:
the tropic of the dryer tumbling clothes.
The round lunar window of the washer.
The kettle in the toaster is a kingfisher
swooping for trout above the river's mirror.

The wash done, the kettle boiled, the sheets
spun and clean, the dryer stops dead.
The silence is a death. It starts to bury
the room in white spaces. She turns to spread
a cloth on the board and irons sheets
in a room white and quiet as a mortuary.

Woman Posing

after the painting Mrs Badham *by Ingres*

She is a housekeeping. A spring cleaning.
A swept, tidied, emptied, kept woman.

Her rimmed hat, its unkempt streamers
neaten to the seams of a collar
frilled and pat as a dressing table,
its pressed lace and ruching hardly able
to hide the solid column of her neck:
reckless fashion masking common sense!

She smirks uneasily at what she's shirking –
sitting on this chair in silly clothes,
posing in a truancy of frills.

There's no repose in her broad knees.
The shawl she shoulders just upholsters her.
She holds the open book like pantry keys.

It's a Woman's World

Our way of life
has hardly changed
since a wheel first
whetted a knife.

Maybe flame
burns more greedily
and wheels are steadier
but we're the same

who milestone
our lives
with oversights –
living by the lights

of the loaf left
by the cash register,
the washing powder
paid for and wrapped,

the wash left wet:
like most historic peoples
we are defined
by what we forget,

by what we will never be –
star-gazers,
fire-eaters.
It's our alibi

for all time:
as far as history goes
we were never
on the scene of the crime.

So when the king's head
gored its basket –
grim harvest –
we were gristing bread

or getting the recipe
for a good soup
to appetise
our gossip.

It's still the same.
By night our windows
moth our children
to the flame

of hearth not history.
And still no page
scores the low music
of our outrage.

Appearances
still reassure:
that woman there
craned to the starry mystery

is merely getting a breath
of evening air,
while this one here –
her mouth

a burning plume –
she's no fire-eater,
just my frosty neighbour
coming home.

Tirade for the Epic Muse

Piston-fisted, engine-headed, blade-faced hag!
They hinged your fingers and you wove their wars,
Unhinged your mind and you told their lies.
They twisted truth; your skein began to fester.
Now they've no use for you. Their wars are won.
But what they've done to you! My muse. My sister.

The hero: Yes, at first you loomed him home,
Blued his view, his sea, blanched his sail,
Staunched his blood, unbandaging your thread
And then you warped him to a wifely bed.
They used him too. Soon, soon his scar
Was sewn and healed to seam another war.

Spooling, spooling newer wars –
Loom and shuttle dressed to kill –
You never noticed, never, fool!
How you were used. You tooled for them.
Your hands were clean, your job was menial –
So you thought – until, until

Slowly, slowly how you changed:
Fingers fixed, a fuselage,
Action-bar, sear and hammer,
Locking block your arms, your hands.
Your eyes were sights. You triggered thread.
You aimed the silk. You made the dead.

They've done with you. Your eyes are dunced.
Your mouth's a bone. You switch and tic.
In my kitchen, in my epic,
Wretch, find peace. You won't notice
My machines. They mist and wink.
But how they'll know you for their own!

The New Pastoral

The first man had flint to spark. He had a wheel
to read his world

I'm in the dark.

I am a lost, last inhabitant –
displaced person
in a pastoral chaos.

All day I listen to
the loud distress, the switch and tick of
new herds.

But I'm no shepherdess.

Can I unbruise these sprouts or clean this mud flesh
till it roots again?
Can I make whole
this lamb's knuckle, butchered from its last crooked suckling?

I could be happy here,
I could be something more than a refugee

were it not for this lamb unsuckled, for the nonstop
switch and tick
telling me

there was a past,
there was a pastoral,
and these chance sights

what are they all
but amnesias of a rite

I danced once on a frieze?

On Renoir's The Grape Pickers

They seem to be what they are harvesting:

rumps, elbows, hips clustering
plumply in the sun; a fuss of shines
wining from the ovals of their elbows.

The brush plucks them from a tied vine.
Such roundness, such a round vintage
of circles, such a work of pure spheres!
Flesh and shadow mesh inside each other.

But not this one: this red-headed woman.
Her skirt's a wave gathered to the weather.
Her eyes are closed. Her hands are loosening.
Her ears are fisted in a dozed listening.
She dreams of stoves, raked leaves, plums.

When she wakes summer will be over.

'Daphne with her thighs in bark'

I have written this

so that,
in the next myth,
my sister will be wiser.

Let her learn from me:

the opposite of passion
is not virtue
but routine.

Look at me

I can be cooking,
making coffee,
scrubbing wood, perhaps,
and back it comes:
the crystalline, the otherwhere,
the wood

where I was
when he began the chase.
And how I ran from him!

Pan-thighed,
satyr-faced he was.

The trees reached out to me.
I silvered and
I quivered. I shook out
my foil of quick leaves.

He snouted past.
What a fool I was!

I shall be here forever,
setting out the tea,
among the coppers and the branching alloys and
the tin shine of this kitchen;
laying saucers on the pine table.

Save face, sister.
Fall. Stumble.
Rut with him.
His rough heat will keep you warm and

you will be better off than me,
with your memories
down the garden,
at the start of March,

unable to keep your eyes
off the chestnut tree –

just the way
it thrusts and hardens.

The Woman Changes Her Skin

How often
in this loneliness,
unlighted
but for the porcelain

brightening
of the bath
have I done this.
Again and again this.

This is the end:
this crêpy
ruche of skin
papering my neck –

elastic when I smile –
and my eyes
a purse of shadows –
it's time for something drastic to be done.

This time
in the shadowy
and woody light
between the bath and blind,

between the day and night,
the same blue
eyeshadow,
rouge and blusher

will mesh
with my fingers
to a weavy
pulse.

In a ringed
coiling,
a convulsion
I will heave

to a sinuous
and final
shining off
of skin:

Look at the hood
I have made
for my eyes,
my head.

And how, quickly,
over my lips
slicked and cold
my tongue flickers.

The Woman Turns Herself into a Fish

Unpod
the bag,
the seed.

Slap
the flanks back.
Flatten

paps.
Make finny
scaled

and chill
the slack
and dimple

of the rump.
Pout
the mouth,

brow the eyes
and now
and now

eclipse
in these hips,
these loins

the moon,
the blood
flux.

It's done.
I turn,
I flab upward

blub-lipped,
hipless
and I am

sexless
shed
of ecstasy,

a pale
swimmer
sequin-skinned,

pearling eggs
screamlessly
in seaweed.

It's what
I set my heart on.
Yet

ruddering
and muscling
in the sunless tons

of new freedoms,
still
I feel

a chill pull,
a brightening,
a light, a light,

and how
in my loomy cold,
my greens,

still
she moons
in me.

The Woman in the Fur Shop

Mole-snouted, in a doze,
The foxes sag like gigolos.
Flaccid. Past it.
But it doesn't matter.
In this light their only role
Is to flatter.

Only in this doorway
Do I hesitate.
A stray.
It never fails,
This spectacle: these women
With their dead heads and tails.

She stands at the glass.
Her hands touch and touch
This skin, her skin,
This fur, her memory.
Memento mori.
And I watch, I watch.

There's nothing
So deranges
As a strange coupling:
The woman turns,
Surprised in wild fur.
Her eyes are stones

And all my body
Is a splayed tail,
A dropped hip
As I lurk away
With ricked hocks
Into an alley.

The Woman as Mummy's Head

Alabastered cream.
Ambergris.
The fragrant simples
Of the eucalyptus tree.
The jellied essences of bees:
They're stuck to me.

I won't put up with it!
And these bandages,
The dirt, the heat,
The wormy litter,
The sheer clutter of it!
But I'm determined now:

I tug: here comes a smile.
Years of smiles. Look.
Lugged and blind. They stink.
They heap at my feet.
The stench!
The dread stench!

Notice now the nose,
Notice with what ease
It strips off and the lips
and the gristle of the chin.
But wait. Wait.
What's this?

I can't hear.
I can't see.
I've done the job too well.
I never thought, I never thought
I could come to this.
I shake in my vacancy.

Is someone there?
I feel you there.
Stand by me. Hand to me
Orchid essences,
The gel of queen bees.
Yes, put in my hands

My shams, my ambers
And my old bandages
So I can poultice
This rabid dark,
This deep, this scream
These absences of me.

A Ballad of Beauty and Time

Plainly came the time
the eucalyptus tree
could not succour me,
nor the honey pot,
the sunshine vitamin.
Not even getting thin.
I had passed my prime.

Then, when bagged ash,
scalded quarts of water,
oil of the lime,
cinders for the skin
and honey all had failed,
I sorted out my money
and went to buy some time.

I knew the right address:
the occult house of shame
where all the women came
shopping for a mouth,
a new nose, an eyebrow
and entered without knocking
and stood as I did now.

A shape with a knife
stooped away from me
cutting something vague –
I couldn't really see –
it might have been a face.
I coughed once and said
– I want a lease of life.

The room was full of masks.
Lines of grins gaping.
A wall of skin stretching.
A chin he had re-worked,
a face he had re-made.
He slit and tucked and cut.
Then straightened from his blade.

'A tuck, a hem' he said –
'I only seam the line,
I only mend the dress.
It wouldn't do for you:
your quarrel's with the weave.
The best I achieve
is just a stitch in time.'

I started out again.
I knew a studio
strewn with cold heels,
closed in marble shock.
I saw the sculptor there
chiselling a nose,
and buttonholed his smock:

'It's all very well
when you have bronzed a woman –
pinioned her and finned
wings on either shoulder.
Anyone can see
she won't get any older.
What good is that to me?'

'See the last of youth
slumming in my skin,
my sham pink mouth.
Here behold your critic –
the threat to your aesthetic
I am the brute proof.
Beauty is not truth.'

'Truth is in our lies –'
he angrily replied.
'This woman fledged in stone,
the centre of all eyes,
her own museum blind:
we sharper with our skills
the arts of compromise.

'And all I have cast
in crystal or in glass,
in lapis or in onyx,
comes from my knowledge when –
above the honest flaw –
to lift and stay my hand
and say "let it stand".'

THE JOURNEY
1987

F<small>OR MY MOTHER</small>

I

I Remember

I remember the way the big windows washed
out the room and the winter darks tinted
it and how, in the brute quiet and aftermath,
an eyebrow waited helplessly to be composed

from the palette with its scarabs of oil
colours gleaming through a dusk leaking from
the iron railings and the ruined evenings of
bombed-out, post-war London; how the easel was

mulberry wood and, porcupining in a jar,
the spines of my mother's portrait brushes
spiked from the dirty turpentine and the face
on the canvas was the scattered fractions

of the face which had come up the stairs
that morning and had taken up position in
the big drawing-room and had been still
and was now gone; and I remember, I remember

I was the interloper who knows both love and fear,
who comes near and draws back, who feels nothing
beyond the need to touch, to handle, to dismantle it,
the mystery; and how in the morning when I came down –

a nine-year-old in high, fawn socks –
the room had been shocked into a glacier
of cotton sheets thrown over the almond
and vanilla silk of the French Empire chairs.

Mise Eire

I won't go back to it –

my nation displaced
into old dactyls,
oaths made
by the animal tallows
of the candle –

land of the Gulf Stream,
the small farm,
the scalded memory,
the songs
that bandage up the history,
the words
that make a rhythm of the crime

where time is time past.
A palsy of regrets.
No. I won't go back.
My roots are brutal:

I am the woman –
a sloven's mix
of silk at the wrists,
a sort of dove-strut
in the precincts of the garrison –

who practises
the quick frictions,
the rictus of delight
and gets cambric for it,
rice-coloured silks.

I am the woman
in the gansy-coat
on board the *Mary Belle*,
in the huddling cold,

holding her half-dead baby to her
as the wind shifts east
and north over the dirty
water of the wharf

mingling the immigrant
guttural with the vowels
of homesickness who neither
knows nor cares that

a new language
is a kind of scar
and heals after a while
into a passable imitation
of what went before.

Self-Portrait on a Summer Evening

Jean-Baptiste Chardin
is painting a woman
in the last summer light.

All summer long
he has been slighting her
in botched blues, tints
half-tones, rinsed neutrals.

What you are watching
is light unlearning itself
an infinite unfrocking of the prism.

Before your eyes
the ordinary life
is being glazed over:
pigments of the bibelot
the cabochon, the water-opal
pearl to the intimate
simple colours of
her ankle-length summer skirt.

Truth makes shift:
the triptych shrinks
to the cabinet picture.

Can't you feel it?
Aren't you chilled by it?
The way the late afternoon
is reduced to detail –

the sky that odd shape of apron –

opaque, scumbled –
the lazulis of the horizon becoming

optical greys
before your eyes
before your eyes
in my ankle-length
summer skirt

crossing between
the garden and the house,
under the whitebeam trees,
keeping an eye on
the length of the grass,
the height of the hedge,
the distance of the children

I am Chardin's woman

edged in reflected light,
hardened by
the need to be ordinary.

The Oral Tradition

I was standing there
at the end of a reading
or a workshop or whatever,
watching people heading
out into the weather,

only half-wondering
what becomes of words,
the brisk herbs of language,
the fragrances we think we sing,
if anything.

We were left behind
in a firelit room
in which the colour scheme
crouched well down –
golds, a sort of dun

a distressed ochre –
and the sole richness was
in the suggestion of a texture
like the low flax gleam
that comes off polished leather.

Two women
were standing in shadow,
one with her back turned.
Their talk was a gesture,
an outstretched hand.

They talked to each other
and words like 'summer'
'birth' 'great-grandmother'
kept pleading with me,
urging me to follow.

'She could feel it coming' –
one of them was saying –
'all the way there,
across the fields at evening
and no one there, God help her

'and she had on a skirt
of cross-woven linen
and the little one
kept pulling at it.
It was nearly night ...'

(Wood hissed and split
in the open grate,
broke apart in sparks,
a windfall of light
in the room's darkness)

'... when she lay down
and gave birth to him
in an open meadow.
What a child that was
to be born without a blemish!'

It had started raining,
the windows dripping, misted.
One moment I was standing
not seeing out,
only half-listening

staring at the night; the next
without warning
I was caught by it:
the bruised summer light,
the musical sub-text

of mauve eaves on lilac
and the laburnum past
and shadow where the lime
tree dropped its bracts
in frills of contrast

where she lay down
in vetch and linen
and lifted up her son
to the archive
they would shelter in:

the oral song
avid as superstition,
layered like an amber in
the wreck of language
and the remnants of a nation.

I was getting out
my coat, buttoning it,
shrugging up the collar.
It was bitter outside,
a real winter's night

and I had distances
ahead of me: iron miles
in trains, iron rails
repeating instances
and reasons; the wheels

singing innuendoes, hints,
outlines underneath
the surface, a sense
suddenly of truth,
its resonance.

Fever

is what remained or what they thought
remained after the ague and the sweats
were over and the shock of wild flowers
at the bedside had been taken away;

is what they tried to shake out of
the crush and dimple of cotton,
the shy dust of a bridal skirt;
is what they beat, lashed, hurt like

flesh as if it were a lack of virtue
in a young girl sobbing her heart out
in a small town for having been seen
kissing by the river; is what they burned

alive in their own back gardens
as if it were a witch and not the full-
length winter gaberdine and breathed again
when the fires went out in charred dew.

My grandmother died in a fever ward,
younger than I am and far from
the sweet chills of a Louth spring –
its sprigged light and its wild flowers –

with five orphan daughters to her name.
Names, shadows, visitations, hints
and a half-sense of half-lives remain.
And nothing else, nothing more unless

I re-construct the soaked-through midnights;
vigils; the histories I never learned
to predict the lyric of; and re-construct
risk; as if silence could become rage,

as if what we lost is a contagion
that breaks out in what cannot be
shaken out from words or beaten out
from meaning and survives to weaken

what is given, what is certain
and burns away everything but this
exact moment of delirium when
someone cries out someone's name.

The Unlived Life

'Listen to me' I said to my neighbour,
'how do you make a hexagon-shape template?'

So we talked about end papers,
cropped circles, block piece-work
while the children shouted and
the texture of synthetics as compared
with the touch of strong cloth
and how they both washed.

'You start out with jest so much caliker' –
Eliza Calvert Hall of Kentucky said –
'that's the predestination
but when it comes to cuttin' out
the quilt, why, you're free to choose.'

Suddenly I could see us
calicoed, overawed, dressed in cotton
at the railroad crossing, watching
the flange-wheeled, steam-driven, iron omen
of another life passing, passing
wondering for a moment what it was
we were missing as we turned for home

to choose
in the shiver of silk and dimity
the unlived life, its symmetry
explored on a hoop with a crewel needle
under the silence of the oil light;

to formalise the terrors of routine
in the algebras of a marriage quilt
on alternate mornings when you knew
that all you owned was what you shared.

It was bed-time for the big children
and long past it for the little ones
as we turned to go
and the height of the season went by us;

tendrils, leaps, gnarls of blossom
asteroids and day-stars of our small world,
the sweet-pea ascending the trellis
the clematis descended
while day backed into night
and separate darks blended the shadows
singling a star out of thin air

as we went in.

Lace

Bent over
the open notebook –

light fades out
making the trees stand out
and my room
at the back
of the house, dark.

In the dusk
I am still
looking for it –
the language that is

lace:

a baroque obligation
at the wrist
of a prince
in a petty court.
Look, just look
at the way he shakes out

the thriftless phrases,
the crystal rhetoric
of bobbined knots

and bosses:
a vagrant drift
of emphasis
to wave away an argument
or frame the hand
he kisses;
which, for all that, is still

what someone
in the corner
of a room,
in the dusk,
bent over
as the light was fading

lost their sight for.

The Bottle Garden

I decanted them – feather mosses, fan-shaped plants,
asymmetric greys in the begonia –
into this globe which shows up how the fern shares
the invertebrate lace of the sea-horse.

The sun is in the bottle garden,
submarine, out of its element
when I come down on a spring morning;
my sweet, greenish, inland underwater.

And in my late thirties, past the middle way,
I can say how did I get here?
I hardly know the way back, still less forward.
Still, if you look for them, there are signs:

Earth stars, rock spleenwort, creeping fig
and English ivy all furled and herded
into the green and cellar wet
of the bottle; well, here they are

here I am a gangling schoolgirl
in the convent library, the April evening outside,
reading the *Aeneid* as the room darkens
to the underworld of the Sixth Book –

the Styx, the damned, the pity and
the improvised poetic of imprisoned meanings;
only half aware of the open weave of harbour lights
and my school blouse riding up at the sleeves.

Suburban Woman: A Detail

I

The chimneys have been swept.
The gardens have their winter cut.
The shrubs are prinked, the hedges gelded.

The last dark shows up the headlights
of the cars coming down the Dublin mountains.

Our children used to think they were stars.

II

This is not the season
when the goddess rose
out of seed, out of wheat,
out of thawed water
and went, distracted and astray,
to find her daughter.

Winter will be soon:
dun pools of rain;
ruddy, addled distances;
winter pinks, tinges and
a first-thing smell of turf
when I take the milk in.

III

Setting out for a neighbour's house
in a denim skirt,

a blouse blended in
by the last light,

I am definite
to start with
but the light is lessening,
the hedge losing its detail,
the path its edge.

Look at me, says the tree.
I was a woman once like you,
full-skirted, human.

Suddenly I am not certain
of the way I came
or the way I will return,
only that something
which may be nothing
more than darkness has begun
softening the definitions
of my body, leaving

the fears and all the terrors
of the flesh shifting the airs
and forms of the autumn quiet

crying 'remember us'.

The Briar Rose

Intimate as underthings
beside the matronly damasks –

the last thing
to go out at night
is the lantern-like, white insistence
of these small flowers;

their camisole glow.

Standing here on the front step
watching wildness break out again

it could be
the unlighted stairway,
I could be
the child I was, opening

a bedroom door
on Irish whiskey, lipstick,
an empty glass,
oyster crêpe-de-Chine

and closing it without knowing why.

The Women

This is the hour I love: the in-between,
neither here-nor-there hour of evening.
The air is tea-coloured in the garden.
The briar rose is spilled crêpe-de-Chine.

This is the time I do my work best,
going up the stairs in two minds,
in two worlds, carrying cloth or glass,
leaving something behind, bringing
something with me I should have left behind.

The hour of change, of metamorphosis,
of shape-shifting instabilities.
My time of sixth sense and second sight
when in the words I choose, the lines I write,
they rise like visions and appear to me:

women of work, of leisure, of the night,
in stove-coloured silks, in lace, in nothing,
with crewel needles, with books, with wide open legs

who fled the hot breath of the god pursuing,
who ran from the split hoof and the thick lips
and fell and grieved and healed into myth,

into me in the evening at my desk
testing the water with a sweet quartet,
the physical force of a dissonance –

the fission of music into syllabic heat –
and getting sick of it and standing up
and going downstairs in the last brightness

into a landscape without emphasis,
light, linear, precisely planned,
a hemisphere of tiered, aired cotton,

a hot terrain of linen from the iron
folded in and over, stacked high
neatened flat, stoving heat and white.

Nocturne

After a friend has gone I like the feel of it:
the house at night. Everyone asleep.
The way it draws in like atmosphere or evening.

One o'clock. A floral teapot and a raisin scone.
A tray waits to be taken down.
The landing light is off. The clock strikes. The cat

comes into his own, mysterious on the stairs,
a black ambivalence around the legs of button-back
chairs, an insinuation to be set beside

the red spoon and the salt-glazed cup,
the saucer with the thick spill of tea
which scalds off easily under the tap. Time

is a tick, a purr, a drop. The spider
on the dining room window has fallen asleep
among complexities as I will once

the doors are bolted and the keys tested
and the switch turned up of the kitchen light
which made outside in the back garden

an electric room – a domestication
of closed daisies, an architecture
instant and improbable.

The Fire in Our Neighbourhood

The sign factory went on fire last night.
Maybe 'factory' is too strong a word.
They painted window-signs there when times
were good, wooden battens, glass, plaster-board.

The paint cans went off like rifle fire.
By the time we heard sirens we were standing
at the windows watching ordinary things –
garden walls, pools of rain – reflecting

violent ornamentation,
our world grown elaborate as if
down-to-earth cloth and wood became
gimp and tatting, guipure and japanning.

Familiar figures became curious shadows.
Everyday men and women were the restless
enigmatic shapes behind glass.
Then the sirens stopped; the end began.

It didn't take long. The fire brigade
turned their hoses on the sawmills where
the rock band practises on Saturdays
with the loud out-of-tune bass guitar.

And the flames went out. The night
belonged to the dark again, to the scent
of rain in the air, to its print on the pavement
and the neighbours who slept through the excitement.

On Holiday

Ballyvaughan.
Peat and salt.
How the wind bawls
across the mountains,
scalds the orchids
of the Burren.

They used to leave milk
out once on these windowsills
to ward away
the child-stealing spirits.

The sheets are damp.
We sleep between the blankets.
The light cotton of the curtains
lets the light in.

You wake first thing
and in your five-year-size
striped nightie you are
everywhere trying everything:
the springs on the bed,
the hinges on the window.

You know your a's and b's
but there's a limit now
to what you'll believe.

When dark comes I leave
a superstitious feast
of wheat biscuits, apples,
orange juice out for you
and wake to find it eaten.

Growing Up

from Renoir's drawing Girlhood

Their two heads, hatted, bowed, mooning
above their waist-high tides of hair
pair hopes.
                        This is the haul and full
of fantasy:
                        full-skirted girls,
a canvas blued and empty with the view
of unschemed space and the anaemic
quick of the pencil picking out
dreams brooding them with womanhood.

They face the future. If they only knew!

There in the distance, bonnetted,
round as the hairline of a child –
indefinite and infinite with hope –
is the horizon, is the past and all
they look forward to is memory.

There and Back

Years ago I left the guest-house
in the first September light
with no sense
I would remember this:

starting up the engine
by the river, picking up
speed on the road
signposted Dublin,

measuring Kilkenny, Carlow, Naas
as distances not places,
yearning for my own
version of the world

every small town was
taking down
its shutters to
and I was still miles from;

until I shut the car door sharp
at eight years ago and you were
with the children,
with their bottles,

at your heels, the little radiances
of their faces turned up,
heliotropic,
to our kiss.

The Wild Spray

It came to me one afternoon in summer –
a gift of long-stemmed flowers in a wet
contemporary sheath of newspapers
which pieced off easily at the sink.

I put them in an ironstone jug
near the window; now years later
I know the names for the flowers
they were but not the shape they made:

The true rose beside the mountain rose,
the muslin finery of asparagus fern,
rosemary, forsythia; something about it was
confined and free in the days that followed

which were the brute, final days of summer –
a consistency of milk about the heat haze,
midges freighting the clear space between
the privet and the hedge, the nights chilling

quickly into stars, the morning breaking late
and on the low table the wild spray
lasted for days, a sweet persuasion,
a random guess becoming a definition.

I have remembered it in a certain way –
displaced yellows and the fluencies
of colours in a jug making a statement of
the unfurnished grace of white surfaces

the way I remember us when we first came here
and had no curtains; the lights on the mountain
that winter were sharp, distant promises
like crocuses through the snowfall of darkness.

We stood together at an upstairs window
enchanted by the patterns in the haphazard,
watching the streetlamp making rain into
a planet of tears near the whitebeam trees.

II

The Journey

for Elizabeth Ryle

Immediately cries were heard. These were the loud wailing of infant souls weeping at the very entrance-way; never had they had their share of life's sweetness for the dark day had stolen them from their mothers' breasts and plunged them to a death before their time.

Virgil, The Aeneid, *Book VI*

And then the dark fell and 'there has never'
I said 'been a poem to an antibiotic:
never a word to compare with the odes on
the flower of the raw sloe for fever

'or the devious Africa-seeking tern
or the protein treasures of the sea-bed.
Depend on it, somewhere a poet is wasting
his sweet uncluttered metres on the obvious

'emblem instead of the real thing.
Instead of sulpha we shall have hyssop dipped
in the wild blood of the unblemished lamb,
so every day the language gets less

'for the task and we are less with the language.'
I finished speaking and the anger faded
and dark fell and the book beside me
lay open at the page Aphrodite

comforts Sappho in her love's duress.
The poplars shifted their music in the garden,
a child startled in a dream,
my room was a mess –

the usual hardcovers, half-finished cups,
clothes piled up on an old chair –
and I was listening out but in my head was
a loosening and sweetening heaviness,

not sleep, but nearly sleep, not dreaming really
but as ready to believe and still
unfevered, calm and unsurprised
when she came and stood beside me

and I would have known her anywhere
and I would have gone with her anywhere
and she came wordlessly
and without a word I went with her

down down down without so much as
ever touching down but always, always
with a sense of mulch beneath us
the way of stairs winding down to a river

and as we went on the light went on
failing and I looked sideways to be certain
it was she, misshapen, musical –
Sappho – the scholiast's nightingale

and down we went, again down
until we came to a sudden rest
beside a river in what seemed to be
an oppressive suburb of the dawn.

My eyes got slowly used to the bad light.
At first I saw shadows, only shadows.
Then I could make out women and children
and, in the way they were, the grace of love.

'Cholera, typhus, croup, diptheria'
she said, 'in those days they racketed
in every backstreet and alley of old Europe.
Behold the children of the plague.'

Then to my horror I could see to each
nipple some had clipped a limpet shape –
suckling darknesses – while others had their arms
weighed down, making terrible pietàs.

She took my sleeve and said to me, 'be careful.
Do not define these women by their work:
not as washerwomen trussed in dust and sweating,
muscling water into linen by the river's edge

'nor as court ladies brailled in silk
on wool and woven with an ivory unicorn
and hung, nor as laundresses tossing cotton,
brisking daylight with lavender and gossip.

'But these are women who went out like you
when dusk became a dark sweet with leaves,
recovering the day, stooping, picking up
teddy bears and rag dolls and tricycles and buckets –

'love's archaeology – and they too like you
stood boot deep in flowers once in summer
or saw winter come in with a single magpie
in a caul of haws, a solo harlequin.'

I stood fixed. I could not reach or speak to them.
Between us was the melancholy river,
the dream water, the narcotic crossing
and they had passed over it, its cold persuasions.

I whispered, 'let me be
let me at least be their witness,' but she said
'what you have seen is beyond speech,
beyond song, only not beyond love;

'remember it, you will remember it'
and I heard her say but she was fading fast
as we emerged under the stars of heaven,
'there are not many of us; you are dear

'and stand beside me as my own daughter.
I have brought you here so you will know forever
the silences in which are our beginnings,
in which we have an origin like water,'

and the wind shifted and the window clasp
opened, banged and I woke up to find
the poetry books stacked higgledy piggledy,
my skirt spread out where I had laid it

nothing was changed; nothing was more clear
but it was wet and the year was late.
The rain was grief in arrears; my children
slept the last dark out safely and I wept.

Envoi

It is Easter in the suburb. Clematis
shrubs the eaves and trellises with pastel.
The evenings lengthen and before the rain
the Dublin mountains become visible.

My muse must be better than those of men
who made theirs in the image of their myth.
The work is half-finished and I have nothing
but the crudest measures to complete it with.

Under the street-lamps the dustbins brighten.
The winter flowering jasmine casts a shadow
outside my window in my neighbour's garden.
These are the things that my muse must know.

She must come to me. Let her come
to be among the donnée, the given.
I need her to remain with me until
the day is over and the song is proven.

Surely she comes, surely she comes to me –
no lizard skin, no paps, no podded womb
about her but a brightening and
the consequences of an April tomb.

What I have done I have done alone.
What I have seen is unverified.
I have the truth and I need the faith.
It is time I put my hand in her side.

If she will not bless the ordinary,
if she will not sanctify the common,
then here I am and here I stay and then am I
the most miserable of women.

III

Listen. This is the Noise of Myth

This is the story of a man and woman
under a willow and beside a weir
near a river in a wooded clearing.
They are fugitives. Intimates of myth.

Fictions of my purpose. I suppose
I shouldn't say that yet or at least
before I break their hearts or save their lives
I ought to tell their story and I will.

When they went first it was winter; cold,
cold through the Midlands and as far West
as they could go. They knew they had to go –
through Meath, Westmeath, Longford,

their lives unravelling like the hours of light –
and then there were lambs under the snow
and it was January, aconite and jasmine
and the hazel yellowing and puce berries on the ivy.

They could not eat where they had cooked,
nor sleep where they had eaten
nor at dawn rest where they had slept.
They shunned the densities

of trees with one trunk and of caves
with one dark and the dangerous embrace
of islands with a single landing place.
And all the time it was cold, cold:

the fields still gardened by their ice,
the trees stitched with snow overnight,
the ditches full; frost toughening lichen,
darning lace into rock crevices.

And then the woods flooded and buds
blunted from the chestnut and the foxglove
put its big leaves out and chaffinches
chinked and flirted in the branches of the ash.

And here we are where we started from –
under a willow and beside a weir
near a river in a wooded clearing.
The woman and the man have come to rest.

Look how light is coming through the ash.
The weir sluices kingfisher blues.
The woman and the willow tree lean forward, forward.
Something is near; something is about to happen;

something more than spring
and less than history. Will we see
hungers eased after months of hiding?
Is there a touch of heat in that light?

If they stay here soon it will be summer; things
returning, sunlight fingering minnowy deeps,
seedy greens, reeds, electing lights
and edges from the river. Consider

legend, self-deception, sin, the sum
of human purpose and its end; remember
how our poetry depends on distance,
aspect: gravity will bend starlight.

Forgive me if I set the truth to rights.
Bear with me if I put an end to this:
She never turned to him; she never leaned
under the sallow-willow over to him.

They never made love; not there; not here;
not anywhere; there was no winter journey;
no aconite, no birdsong and no jasmine,
no woodland and no river and no weir.

Listen. This is the noise of myth. It makes
the same sound as shadow. Can you hear it?
Daylight greys in the preceptories.
Her head begins to shine

pivoting the planets of a harsh nativity.
They were never mine. This is mine.
This sequence of evicted possibilities.
Displaced facts. Tricks of light. Reflections.

Invention. Legend. Myth. What you will.
The shifts and fluencies are infinite.
The moving parts are marvellous. Consider
how the bereavements of the definite

are easily lifted from our heroine.
She may or she may not. She was or wasn't
by the water at his side as dark
waited above the Western countryside.

O consolations of the craft.
How we put
the old poultices on the old sores,
the same mirrors to the old magic. Look.

The scene returns. The willow sees itself
drowning in the weir and the woman
gives the kiss of myth her human heat.
Reflections. Reflections. He becomes her lover.

The old romances make no bones about it.
The long and short of it. The end and the beginning.
The glories and the ornaments are muted.
And when the story ends the song is over.

An Irish Childhood in England: 1951

The bickering of vowels on the buses,
the clicking thumbs and the big hips of
the navy-skirted ticket collectors with
their crooked seams brought it home to me:
Exile. Ration-book pudding.
Bowls of dripping and the fixed smile
of the school pianist playing 'Iolanthe',
'Land of Hope and Glory' and 'John Peel'.

I didn't know what to hold, to keep.
At night, filled with some malaise
of love for what I'd never known I had,
I fell asleep and let the moment pass.
The passing moment has become a night
of clipped shadows, freshly painted houses,
the garden eddying in dark and heat,
my children half-awake, half-asleep.

Airless, humid dark. Leaf-noise.
The stirrings of a garden before rain.
A hint of storm behind the risen moon.
We are what we have chosen. Did I choose to? –
in a strange city, in another country,
on nights in a north-facing bedroom,
waiting for the sleep that never did
restore me as I'd hoped to what I'd lost –

let the world I knew become the space
between the words that I had by heart
and all the other speech that always was
becoming the language of the country that
I came to in nineteen-fifty-one:
barely-gelled, a freckled six-year-old,
overdressed and sick on the plane
when all of England to an Irish child

was nothing more than what you'd lost and how:
was the teacher in the London convent who
when I produced 'I amn't' in the classroom
turned and said – 'you're not in Ireland now'.

Fond Memory

It was a school where all the children wore darned worsted;
where they cried – or almost all – when the Reverend Mother
announced at lunch-time that the King had died

peacefully in his sleep. I dressed in wool as well,
ate rationed food, played English games and learned
how wise the Magna Carta was, how hard the Hanoverians

had tried, the measure and complexity of verse,
the hum and score of the whole orchestra.
At three o'clock I caught two buses home

where sometimes in the late afternoon
at a piano pushed into a corner of the playroom
my father would sit down and play the slow

lilts of Tom Moore while I stood there trying
not to weep at the cigarette smoke stinging up
from between his fingers and – as much as I could think –

I thought this is my country, was, will be again,
this upward-straining song made to be
our safe inventory of pain. And I was wrong.

Canaletto in the National Gallery of Ireland

Something beating in
making pain and attention –
a heat still
livid on the skin
is the might-have-been:

the nation, the city
which fell
for want of
the elevation in
this view of the Piazza,

its everyday light
making it everyone's
remembered city:
airs and shadows,
cambered distances.

I remember
a city like this –
the static coral
of reflected brick
in its river.

I envy these
pin-pointed citizens
their solid ease,
their lack of any need
to come and see

the beloved republic
raised
and saved
and scalded into
something measurable.

The Emigrant Irish

Like oil lamps we put them out the back,

of our houses, of our minds. We had lights
better than, newer than and then

a time came, this time and now
we need them. Their dread, makeshift example.

They would have thrived on our necessities.
What they survived we could not even live.
By their lights now it is time to
imagine how they stood there, what they stood with,
that their possessions may become our power.

Cardboard. Iron. Their hardships parcelled in them.
Patience. Fortitude. Long-suffering
in the bruise-coloured dusk of the New World.

And all the old songs. And nothing to lose.

Tirade for the Lyric Muse

You're propped and swabbed and bedded.
I could weep.
There's a stench of snipped flesh
and tubed blood.
I've come to see if beauty is skin deep.

Mongrel features.
Tainted lint and cotton.
Sutures from the lip to ear to brow.
They've patched your wrinkles
and replaced your youth.
It may be beauty
but it isn't truth.

You are the victim of a perfect crime.
You have no sense of time.
You never had.
You never dreamed he could be so cruel.
Which is why you lie back
shocked in cambric,
slacked in bandages
and blubbing gruel.
My white python writhing your renewal!

I loved you once.
It seemed so right, so neat.
The moon, the month, the flower, the kiss –
there wasn't anything that wouldn't fit.
The ends were easy
and the means were short
when you and I were lyric and elect.
Shall I tell you what we overlooked?

You in this bed.
You with your snout,
your seams, your stitches
and your sutured youth.
You,
you with your smocked mouth
are what your songs left out.

We still have time.
Look in the glass.
Time is the flaw.
Truth is the crystal.

We have been sisters
in the crime.
Let us be sisters
in the physic:

Listen.
Bend your darned head.
Turn your good ear.
Share my music.

The Woman takes her Revenge on the Moon

Claret. Plum. Cinnabar.
The damask of the peach.
The flame and sweet
carmine of late berries.
The orchard colours of the morning –

I am learning them.
I streak ochres on my cheeks.
This is my make-up box.
This is how I own
the tone secrets of the dawn.

It takes skill
to make my skin
a facsimile
of absolute light,
of scarlet turning into carmine.

Once I start
I lose all sense
of time, of space,
of clarity, of will.
I mix to kill.

Orange madder.
The magenta tint.
I am perfecting it.
It must be excellent
or she won't fall for it.

I fresh the pearly wet
across my face.
I rouge the flesh.
I spread and flush the red.
The trap is set.

I walk out
in the evening air.
Early, early
in the clear evening.
I raise my head like a snare.

There it is.
I can feel it –
the pleasure of it! –
the dun slither,
the hysteric of her white

expression, its surprise
as she drowns,
as she douses
in my face,
m my sunrise.

The Glass King

Isabella of Bavaria married Charles VI of France in 1385. In later years his madness took the form of believing he was made from glass.

When he is ready he is raised and carried
among his vaporish plants; the palms and ferns flex;
they almost bend; you'd almost think they were going to kiss him;
and so they might; but she will not, his wife,

no she can't kiss the lips in case he splinters
into a million Bourbons, mad pieces.
What can she do with him – her daft prince?
His nightmares are the Regency of France.

Yes, she's been through it all, his Bavaroise,
blub-hipped and docile, urgent to be needed –
from churching to milk fever, from tongue-tied princess
to the queen of a mulish king – and now this.

They were each other's fantasy in youth.
No splintering at all about that mouth
when they were flesh and muscle, woman and man,
fire and kindling. See that silk divan?

Enough said. Now the times themselves
are his asylum: these are the Middle Ages, sweet
and savage era of the saving grace; indulgences
are two a penny; under the stonesmith's hand

stone turns into lace. I need his hand now.
Outside my window October soaks the stone;
you can hear it; you'd almost think
the brick was drinking it; the rowan drips

and history waits. Let it wait. I want
no elsewheres: the clover-smelling, stove-warm
air of autumn catches cold; the year turns;
the leaves fall; the poem hesitates:

If we could see ourselves, not as we do –
in mirrors, self-deceptions, self-regardings –
but as we ought to be and as we have been:
poets, lute-stringers, makyres and abettors

of our necessary art, soothsayers of the ailment
and disease of our times, sweet singers,
truth tellers, intercessors for self-knowledge –
what would we think of these fin-de-siècle

half-hearted penitents we have become
at the sick-bed of the century: hand-wringing
elegists with an ill-concealed greed
for the inheritance?
                My prince, demented

in a crystal past, a lost France, I elect you emblem
and ancestor of our lyric: it fits you like a glove –
doesn't it? – the part; untouchable, outlandish,
esoteric, inarticulate and out of reach

of human love: studied every day by your wife,
an ordinary honest woman out of place
in all this, wanting nothing more than the man
she married, all her sorrows in her stolid face.

OUTSIDE HISTORY

1990

FOR KEVIN CASEY

I Object Lessons

The Black Lace Fan My Mother Gave Me

It was the first gift he ever gave her,
buying it for five francs in the Galeries
in pre-war Paris. It was stifling.
A starless drought made the nights stormy.

They stayed in the city for the summer.
They met in cafés. She was always early.
He was late. That evening he was later.
They wrapped the fan. He looked at his watch.

She looked down the Boulevard des Capucines.
She ordered more coffee. She stood up.
The streets were emptying. The heat was killing.
She thought the distance smelled of rain and lightning.

These are wild roses, appliqued on silk by hand,
darkly picked, stitched boldly, quickly.
The rest is tortoiseshell and has the reticent,
clear patience of its element. It is

a worn-out, underwater bullion and it keeps,
even now, an inference of its violation.
The lace is overcast as if the weather
it opened for and offset had entered it.

The past is an empty café terrace.
An airless dusk before thunder. A man running.
And no way now to know what happened then –
none at all – unless, of course, you improvise:

The blackbird on this first sultry morning,
in summer, finding buds, worms, fruit,
feels the heat. Suddenly she puts out her wing –
the whole, full, flirtatious span of it.

The Rooms of Other Women Poets

I wonder about you: whether the blue abrasions
of daylight, falling as dusk across your page,

make you reach for the lamp. I sometimes think
I see that gesture in the way you use language.

And whether you think, as I do, that wild flowers
dried and fired on the ironstone rim of

the saucer underneath your cup, are a sign of
a savage, old calligraphy: you will not have it.

The chair you use, for instance, may be cane
soaked and curled in spirals, painted white

and eloquent, or iron mesh and the table
a horizon of its own on plain, deal trestles,

bearing up unmarked, steel-cut foolscap,
a whole quire of it; when you leave I know

you look at them and you love their air of
unaggressive silence as you close the door.

The early summer, its covenant, its grace,
is everywhere: even shadows have leaves.

Somewhere you are writing or have written in
a room you came to as I come to this

room with honeyed corners, the interior sunless,
the windows shut but clear so I can see

the bay windbreak, the laburnum hang fire, feel
the ache of things ending in the jasmine darkening early.

Object Lessons

It was yours.
Your coffee mug. Black,
with a hunting scene on the side
(cruel theatre as the kettle poured).
Together, we unpacked it
in the new house.

A hunting scene:
Dogs. Hawking. Silk.
Linen spread out in a meadow.
Pitchers of wine clouding in the shadow
of beech trees. Buttermilk.
A huntsman.

A wild rabbit.
A thrush ready to sing.
A lady smiling as the huntsman kissed her:
the way land looks before disaster
strikes or suffering
becomes a habit

was not a feature
of the history we knew. Now
it opened out before us, bright
as our curtainless October nights
whose street-lit glow
was second nature. Or

those mornings
we drank coffee
and shared cake in a kitchen full of
chaos, before we knew the details of
this pastoral were merely
veiled warnings

of the shiver
of presentiment with which
we found the broken pieces of
the sparrow hawk and the kisses of
the huntsman, the pitcher
and the thrush's never

to-be-finished
aria, an untouched meal,
and the lady and the hunting horn
on the floorboards you and I had sworn
to sand down and seal
with varnish.

On the Gift of The Birds of America
by John James Audubon

What you have given me is, of course, elegy: the red-shouldered
hawk in among these scattering partridges,
flustered at

such a descent, and the broad-winged one poised on the branch
of a pignut, and the pine siskin and the wren are
an inference

we follow in the plummet of the tern which appears to be,
from this angle anyway, impossibly fragile and
if we imagine

the franchise of light these camphor-coloured wings opened out
once with and are at such a loss for now,
then surely this

is the nature and effect of elegy: the celebration of an element
which absence has revealed: it is
our earthliness

we love as we look at them, which we fear to lose, which we need
this re-phrasing of the air,
of the ocean

to remind us of: that evening, late in May, the Clare hills were
ghostly with hawthorn. Two swans flew over us.
I can still hear

the musical insistence of their wings as they came in past
the treetops, near the lake; and we looked up,
rooted to the spot.

The Game

Outside my window an English spring was
summoning home its birds and a week-long fog
was tattering into wisps and rags and at last
I could see the railings when I looked out.

I was a child in a north-facing bedroom in
a strange country. I lay awake listening to
quarrelling and taffeta creaking and the clattering
of queens and aces on the inlaid card table.

I played a game: I hid my face in the pillow
and put my arms around it until they thickened.
Then I was following the thaw northward and the air
was blonde with frost and sunshine and below me

was only water and the shadow of flight in it
and the shape of wings under it, and in the hours
before morning I would be drawn down and drawn
down and there would be no ground under me

and no safe landing in the dawn breaking on
a room with sharp corners and surfaces on which
the red-jacketed and cruel-eyed fractions of chance
lay scattered where the players had abandoned them.

Later on I would get up and go to school in
the scalded light which fog leaves behind it;
and pray for the King in chapel and feel dumbly for
the archangels trapped in their granite hosannahs.

The Shadow Doll

This was sent to the bride-to-be in Victorian times, by her dressmaker.
It consisted in a porcelain doll, under a dome of glass, modelling
the proposed wedding dress.

They stitched blooms from ivory tulle
to hem the oyster gleam of the veil.
They made hoops for the crinoline.

Now, in summary and neatly sewn –
a porcelain bride in an airless glamour –
the shadow doll survives its occasion.

Under glass, under wraps, it stays
even now, after all, discreet about
visits, fevers, quickenings and lusts

and just how, when she looked at
the shell-tone spray of seed pearls,
the bisque features, she could see herself

inside it all, holding less than real
stephanotis, rose petals, never feeling
satin rise and fall with the vows

I kept repeating on the night before –
astray among the cards and wedding gifts –
the coffee pots and the clocks and

the battered tan case full of cotton
lace and tissue-paper, pressing down, then
pressing down again. And then, locks.

The River

You brought me
    to the mouth of a river
in mid–October
    when the swamp maples
were saw-toothed and blemished.
    I remember

how strange it felt –
    not having any
names for the red oak
    and the rail
and the slantways plunge
    of the osprey.

What we said was less
    than what we saw.
What we saw was
    a duck boat, slowly
passing us, a hunter and
    his spaniel, and

his gun poised,
    and, in the distance,
the tips of the wild
    rice drowning in
that blue which raids and
    excludes light.

Mountain Time

Time is shadowless there: mornings re-occur
only as enchantments, only as time for her

to watch berries ripen by on the mountain ash;
for him, at a short distance from her, to catch fish.

Afterwards, darkness will be only what is left of
a mouth after kissing or a hand laced in a hand;

a branch; a river; will be what is lost of words
as they turn to silences and then to sleep. Yet

when they leave the mountain what he will remember is
the rowan trees: that blemish, that scarlet. She will think of

the arc of the salmon after sudden capture –
its glitter a larceny of daylight on slate.

The Latin Lesson

Easter light in the convent garden.
The eucalyptus tree glitters in it.
A bell rings for
the first class.

Today the Sixth Book of the *Aeneid*.
An old nun calls down the corridor.
Manners, girls. Where
are your manners?

Last night in his Lenten talk
the local priest asked us to remember
everything is put here
for a purpose:

even eucalyptus leaves are suitable
for making oil from to steep wool in,
to sweeten our blankets
and gaberdines.

My forefinger crawls on the lines.
A storm light comes in from the bay.
How beautiful the words
look, how

vagrant and strange on the page
before we crush them for their fragrance
and crush them again
to discover

the pathway to hell and that these
shadows in their shadow-bodies,
chittering and mobbing
on the far

shore, signalling their hunger for
the small usefulness of a life, are
the dead. And how
before the bell

will I hail the black keel and flatter the dark
boatman and cross the river and still
keep a civil tongue
in my head?

Bright-Cut Irish Silver

I take it down
from time to time, to feel
the smooth path of silver meet the cicatrice of skill.

These scars, I tell myself, are learned.

This gift for wounding an artery of rock
was passed on from father to son, to the father
of the next son;

is an aptitude
for injuring earth while inferring it in curves and surfaces;

is this cold potency which has come,
by time and chance,

into my hands.

We Were Neutral in the War

This warm, late summer there is so much
to get in. The ladder waits by the crab apple tree.
The greenhouse is rank with the best
Irish tomatoes. Pears are ripening.

Your husband frowns at dinner, has no time
for the baby who has learned to crease three
fingers and wave 'day-day'. This is serious,
he says. This could be what we all feared.

You pierce a sequin with a needle.
You slide it down single-knotted thread
until it lies with all the others in
a puzzle of brightness. Then another and another one.

Let the green and amber marrows rise up
and beat against it and the crab apples and
the damson-coloured pram by the back
wall: you will not sew them into it.

The wooden ledge of the conservatory
faces south. Row on row,
the pears are laid out there, are hard
and then yellow and then yellow with

a rosiness. You leave them out of it.
They will grow soft and bruised at the top
and rot, all in one afternoon. The light,
which made them startling, you will use.

On the breakfast table the headlines are
telling of a city under threat where
you mixed cheese with bitter fennel and
fell in love over demitasse. Afterwards,

you walked by the moonlit river and stopped
and looked down. A glamorous circumference is
spinning on your needle, is
that moon in satin water making

the same peremptory demands on
the waves of the Irish sea and as each
salt-window opens to reveal
a weather of agates, you will stitch that in

with the orchard colours of the first preserves
you make from the garden. You move the jars from
the pantry to the windowsill where
you can see them: winter jewels.

The night he comes to tell you this is war
you wait for him to put on his dinner jacket.
The party is tonight.
The streets are quiet. Dublin is at peace.

The talk is of death but you take
the hand of the first man who asks you.
You dance the fox-trot, the two-step,
the quick-step,

in time to the music. Exclusions
glitter at your hips and past and future are
the fended-off and far-fetched
in waltz time below your waist.

II Outside History
A sequence

I *The Achill Woman*

She came up the hill carrying water.
She wore a half-buttoned, wool cardigan,
a tea-towel round her waist.

She pushed the hair out of her eyes with
her free hand and put the bucket down.

The zinc-music of the handle on the rim
tuned the evening. An Easter moon rose.
In the next-door field a stream was
a fluid sunset; and then, stars.

I remember the cold rosiness of her hands.
She bent down and blew on them like broth.
And round her waist, on a white background,
in coarse, woven letters, the words 'glass cloth'.

And she was nearly finished for the day.
And I was all talk, raw from college –
week-ending at a friend's cottage
with one suitcase and the set text
of the Court poets of the Silver Age.

We stayed putting down time until
the evening turned cold without warning.
She said goodnight and started down the hill.

The grass changed from lavender to black.
The trees turned back to cold outlines.
You could taste frost

but nothing now can change the way I went
indoors, chilled by the wind
and made a fire
and took down my book
and opened it and failed to comprehend

the harmonies of servitude,
the grace music gives to flattery
and language borrows from ambition –

and how I fell asleep
oblivious to

the planets clouding over in the skies,
the slow decline of the spring moon,
the songs crying out their ironies.

II   A False Spring

Alders are tasselled.
Flag-iris is already out on the canal.

From my window I can see
the College gardens, crocuses stammering
in pools of rain, plum blossom
on the branches.

I want to find her,
the woman I once was,
who came out of that reading-room
in a hard January, after studying
Aeneas in the underworld,

how his old battle-foes spotted him there –

how they called and called and called
only to have it be
a yell of shadows, an O vanishing in
the polished waters
and the topsy-turvy seasons of hell –

her mind so frail her body was its ghost.

I want to tell her she can rest,
she is embodied now.

But narcissi,
opening too early,
are all I find.
I hear the bad sound of these south winds,
the rain coming from some region which has lost sight
of our futures, leaving us
nothing to look forward to except
what one serious frost can accomplish.

III   The Making of an Irish Goddess

Ceres went to hell
with no sense of time.

When she looked back
all that she could see was

the arteries of silver in the rock,
the diligence of rivers always at one level,
wheat at one height,
leaves of a single colour,
the same distance in the usual light;

a seasonless, unscarred earth.

But I need time –
my flesh and that history –
to make the same descent.

In my body,
neither young now nor fertile,
and with the marks of childbirth
still on it,

in my gestures –
the way I pin my hair to hide
the stitched, healed blemish of a scar –
must be

an accurate inscription
of that agony:

the failed harvests,
the fields rotting to the horizon,
the children devoured by their mothers
whose souls, they would have said,
went straight to hell,
followed by their own.

There is no other way:

myth is the wound we leave
in the time we have

which in my case is this
March evening
at the foothills of the Dublin mountains,
across which the lights have changed all day,

holding up my hand,
sickle-shaped, to my eyes
to pick out
my own daughter from
all the other children in the distance;

her back turned to me.

IV White Hawthorn in the West of Ireland

I drove West
in the season between seasons.
I left behind suburban gardens.
Lawnmowers. Small talk.

Under low skies, past splashes of coltsfoot,
I assumed
the hard shyness of Atlantic light
and the superstitious aura of hawthorn.

All I wanted then was to fill my arms with
sharp flowers,
to seem, from a distance, to be part of
that ivory, downhill rush. But I knew,

I had always known
the custom was
not to touch hawthorn.
Not to bring it indoors for the sake of

the luck
such constraint would forfeit –
a child might die, perhaps, or an unexplained
fever speckle heifers. So I left it

stirring on those hills
with a fluency
only water has. And, like water, able
to re-define land. And free to seem to be –

for anglers,
and for travellers astray in
the unmarked lights of a May dusk –
the only language spoken in those parts.

V Daphne Heard with Horror the Addresses
of the God

It was early summer. Already
the conservatory was all steam and greenness.
I would have known the stephanotis by
its cut-throat sweetness anywhere.
We drank tea. You were telling me
a story you had heard as a child,
about the wedding of a local girl,
long ago, and a merchant from Argyll.

I thought the garden looked so at ease.
The roses were beginning on one side.
The laurel hedge was nothing but itself,
and all of it so free of any need
for nymphs, goddesses, wounded presences –
the fleet river-daughters who took root
and can be seen in the woods in
unmistakable shapes of weeping.

You were still speaking. By the time
I paid attention they were well married:
the bridegroom had his bride on the ship.
The sails were ready to be set. You said
small craft went with her to the ship and,
as it sailed out, well-wishers
took in armfuls, handfuls, from the boats
white roses and threw them on the water.

We cleared up then, saying how
the greenfly needed spraying, the azaleas
were over; and you went inside. I
stayed in the heat looking out at
the garden in its last definition.
Freshening and stirring. A suggestion,
behind it all, of darkness. In the shadow,
beside the laurel hedge, its gesture.

VI The Photograph on My Father's Desk

It could be
any summer afternoon.

The sun is warm on
the fruitwood garden seat.
Fuchsia droops.
Thrushes move to get
windfalls underneath the crab apple tree.

The woman
holds her throat like a wound.

She wears
mutton-coloured gaberdine with
a scum of lace
just above her boot

which is pointed at
this man coming down the path with
his arms wide open. Laughing.

The garden fills up
with a burned silence.

The talk has stopped.
The spoon which just now
jingled at the rim of the lemonade jug
is still.

And the shrubbed lavender
will find
neither fragrance nor muslin.

VII We Are Human History.
We Are Not Natural History.

At twilight in
the shadow of the poplars
the children found a swarm of wild bees.

It was late summer and I knew as
they came shouting in that, yes,
this evening had been singled out by

a finger pointing at trees,
the inland feel of that greenness,
the sugar-barley iron of a garden chair

and children still bramble-height
and fretful from the heat and a final
brightness stickle-backing that particular

patch of grass across which light
was short-lived and elegiac as
the view from a train window of

a station parting, all tears. And this,
this I thought, is how it will have been
chosen from those summer evenings

which under the leaves of the poplars –
striped dun and ochre, simmering over
the stashed-up debris of old seasons –

a swarm of wild bees is making use of.

VIII An Old Steel Engraving

Look.
The figure in the foreground breaks his fall with
one hand. He cannot die.
The river cannot wander
into the shadows to be dragged by willows.
The passer-by is scared witless. He cannot escape.
He cannot stop staring at
this hand which can barely raise
the patriot
above the ground which is
the origin and reason for it all.

More closely now:
at the stillness of unfinished action in
afternoon heat, at the spaces on the page. They widen
to include us:
we have found

the country of our malediction where
nothing can move until we find the word,
nothing can stir until we say this is

what happened and is happening and history
is one of us who turns away
while the other is
turning the page.

Is this river which
moments ago must have flashed the morse
of a bayonet thrust. And is moving on.

IX *In Exile*

The German girls who came to us that winter and
the winter after and who helped my mother fuel
the iron stove and arranged our clothes in wet
thicknesses on the wooden rail after tea was over,

spoke no English, understood no French. They were
sisters from a ruined city and they spoke rapidly
in their own tongue: syllables in which pain was
radical, integral; and with what sense of injury

the language angled for an unhurt kingdom – for
the rise, curve, kill and swift return to the wrist,
to the hood – I never knew. To me they were the sounds
of evening only, of the cold, of the Irish dark and

continuous with all such recurrences: the drizzle in
the lilac, the dusk always at the back door, like
the tinkers I was threatened with, the cat inching
closer to the fire with its screen of clothes, where

I am standing in the stone-flagged kitchen; there are
bleached rags, perhaps, and a pot of tea on the stove.
And I see myself, four years of age and looking up,
storing such music – guttural, hurt to the quick –

as I hear now, forty years on and far from where
I heard it first. Among these salt-boxes, marshes and
the glove-tanned colours of the sugar-maples, in
this New England town at the start of winter, I am

so much south of it: the soft wet, the light and
those early darks which strengthen the assassin's
hand; and hide the wound. Here, in this scalding air,
my speech will not heal. I do not want it to heal.

X   *We Are Always Too Late*

Memory
is in two parts.

First, the re-visiting:

the way even now I can see
those lovers at the café table. She is weeping.

It is New England, breakfast-time, winter. Behind her,
outside the picture window, is
a stand of white pines.

New snow falls and the old,
losing its balance in the branches,
showers down,
adding fractions to it. Then

the re-enactment. Always that.
I am getting up, pushing away
coffee. Always, I am going towards her.

The flush and scald is
to her forehead now, and back down to her neck.

I raise one hand. I am pointing to
those trees, I am showing her our need for these
beautiful upstagings of
what we suffer by
what survives. And she never even sees me.

XI *What We Lost*

It is a winter afternoon.
The hills are frozen. Light is failing.
The distance is a crystal earshot.
A woman is mending linen in her kitchen.

She is a countrywoman.
Behind her cupboard doors she hangs sprigged,
stove-dried lavender in muslin.
Her letters and mementoes and memories

are packeted in satin at the back with
gaberdine and worsted and
the cambric she has made into bodices;
the good tobacco silk for Sunday Mass.

She is sewing in the kitchen.
The sugar-feel of flax is in her hands.
Dusk. And the candles brought in then.
One by one. And the quiet sweat of wax.

There is a child at her side.
The tea is poured, the stitching put down.
The child grows still, sensing something of importance.
The woman settles and begins her story.

Believe it, what we lost is here in this room
on this veiled evening.
The woman finishes. The story ends.
The child, who is my mother, gets up, moves away.

In the winter air, unheard, unshared,
the moment happens, hangs fire, leads nowhere.
The light will fail and the room darken,
the child fall asleep and the story be forgotten.

The fields are dark already.
The frail connections have been made and are broken.
The dumb-show of legend has become language,
is becoming silence and who will know that once

words were possibilities and disappointments,
were scented closets filled with love-letters
and memories and lavender hemmed into muslin,
stored in sachets, aired in bed-linen;

and travelled silks and the tones of cotton
tautened into bodices, subtly shaped by breathing;
were the rooms of childhood with their griefless peace,
their hands and whispers, their candles weeping brightly?

XII   Outside History

There are outsiders, always. These stars —
these iron inklings of an Irish January,
whose light happened

thousands of years before
our pain did: they are, they have always been
outside history.

They keep their distance. Under them remains
a place where you found
you were human, and

a landscape in which you know you are mortal.
And a time to choose between them.
I have chosen:

out of myth into history I move to be
part of that ordeal
whose darkness is

only now reaching me from those fields,
those rivers, those roads clotted as
firmaments with the dead.

How slowly they die
as we kneel beside them, whisper in their ear.
And we are too late. We are always too late.

III   Distances

Nights of Childhood

My mother kept a stockpot –

garlic cloves, bones,
rinds, pearl onions and the lacy spine and eyes
of a trout went into it.

When the window cleared, the garden showed
beyond the lemon balm,
through the steam,
cats.

Bucking. Rutting.
All buttocks and stripes.
Up on the wall and wild, they made the garden wild –
for all the gelded shrubs and the careful stemming
on trellises, of a bushed-out, pastel clematis.

One summer night I went out to them.
I looked up. Their eyes looked back –

not the colour of fields or kale,
the available greens,
but jade-cold
and with a closed-in chill I was used to –

lucid as a nursery rhyme and as hard to fathom,
revealed by rhythm, belied by theme
never forgotten

in those nights of childhood,
in a roomful of breathing, under wartime sheeting.

Outside, the screams and stridency of mating.

The Carousel in the Park

Find it.

Down the park walks, on the path leading
past the sycamores.
There through the trees –

nasturtium rumps, breasts plunging,
lime and violet manes
painted on
what was once the same as now littered
russet on their petrified advance.

Find the sun
in the morning rising later,
the chilled afternoons getting shorter and
after dusk, in the lake, in the park,
the downtown city windows scattering
a galaxy of money
in the water.

And winter coming:

the man-handled indigo necks flexing and
the flared noses
and the heads with their quiffed carving.

And the walks leafless and
the squirrels gone,
the sycamores bare and the lake frozen.

Find the child,
going high and descending there. Up and down.
Up, down again.
Her mittens bright as finger-paints and holding fast
to a crust of weather now: twelve years of age in
a thigh-length coat,
unable to explain a sense of ease in

those safe curves, that seasonless canter.

Contingencies

Waiting in the kitchen for power cuts,
on this wet night, sorting candles,
feeling the tallow,
brings back to me
the way women spoke in my childhood –

with a sweet mildness in front of company,
or with a private hunger in whispered kisses,
or with the crisis-bright words
which meant

you and you alone were their object –

'Stop that.' 'Wait till I get you.'
'Dry those tears.'

I stand the candles in jam jars
lined in a row on the table,
scalded and dried with a glass cloth;

which all last summer were crammed with
the fruits of neighbourly gardens.

Stoned plums and damsons. Loganberries.

Spring at the Edge of the Sonnet

Late March and I'm still lighting fires –

last night's frost which killed the new
shoots of ivy in the terracotta churn,
has turned the fields of wheat and winter barley

to icy slates on the hills rising
outside the windows of our living room.

Still, there are signs of change. Soon,
the roofs of cars, which last month were
oracles of ice and unthawed dawns,

will pass by, veiled in blooms from
the wild plum they parked under overnight.

Last night, as I drove from town,
the dark was in and the lovers were
out in doorways, using them as windbreaks,
making shadows seem nothing more than

sweet exchequers for a homeless kiss.

Our Origins Are in the Sea

I live near the coast. On these summer nights
the dog-star rises somewhere near the hunter,
near the sun. I stand at the edge of our grass.

I do not connect them: once they were connected –
the fixity of stars and unruly salt water –
by sailors with an avarice for landfall.

And this is land. The way the whitebeams will
begin their fall to an alluvial earth and
a bicycle wheel is spinning on it, proves that.

From where I stand the sea is just a rumour.
The stars are put out by our streetlamp. Light
and seawater are well separated. And how little

survives of the sea-captain in his granddaughter
is everywhere apparent. Such things get lost:
He drowned in the Bay of Biscay. I never saw him.

I turn to go in. The hills are indistinct.
The coast is near and darkening. The stars are clearer.
The grass and the house are lapped in shadow.

And the briar rose is rigged in the twilight,
the way I imagine sails used to be –
lacy and stiff together, a frigate of ivory.

Midnight Flowers

I go down step by step.
The house is quiet, full of trapped heat and sleep.
In the kitchen everything is still.
Nothing is distinct; there is no moon to speak of.

I could be undone every single day by
paradox or what they call in the countryside
blackthorn winter,
when hailstones come with the first apple blossom.

I turn a switch and the garden grows.
A whole summer's work in one instant!
I press my face to the glass. I can see
shadows of lilac, of fuchsia; a dark likeness of blackcurrant:

little clients of suddenness, how sullen they are at
the margins of the light.
They need no rain, they have no roots.
I reach out a hand; they are gone.

When I was a child a snapdragon was
held an inch from my face. Look, a voice said, this
is the colour of your hair. And there it was, my head,
a pliant jewel in the hands of someone else.

Doorstep Kisses

The white iron of the garden chair is
the only thing dusk makes clearer.

I have stumbled on
the last days of summer in the last hour of light.

If I stay here long enough I may become –
since everything else around me is –

the sum of small gestures, choices,
losses in the air so fractional
they could be

fragrances which just fell from it –

a musk of buddleia, perhaps, or this fuchsia
with the drip,
drip of Whitby jet fringing
an old rose printed shawl I saw once

which swung out and over my shoulders,
flinging out its scent
of early chills and doorstep kisses.

A Different Light

Talking just like this late at night
all depends on a sense of mystery;
the same things in a different light.

Your whiskey glass and the watercolour
just off-centre are
part of this. The electric pallor

of that apple, also. And the slow
arc of an indoor palm, the vase beside it blooming
with shadows. Do you remember how

the power cuts caught us unawares?
No candles and no torch. It was high
summer. A soft brightness clung in the poplars,

for hours it seemed. When it went out,
everything we knew how
to look for had disappeared. And when light

came back, it came back as noise:
the radio; the deep freeze singing.
Afterwards we talked of it for days –

how it felt at the upstairs window,
to stand and watch and still miss the moment
of gable ends and rooftops beginning

to be re-built. And that split second when
you and I were, from a distance,
a neighbourhood on the verge of definition.

Hanging Curtains with an Abstract Pattern
in a Child's Room

I chose these for you –
not the precinct of the unicorn, nor

the half-torn
singlet of a nursery rhyme prince, but

the signals of enigma:
Ellipse. Triangle. A music of ratio.

Draw these lines
against a winter dusk. Let them stand in for

frost on the spider's web and on
bicycle sheds.

Observe
how the season enters pure line

like a soul: all the signs we know
are only ways

of coming to our senses.
I can see

the distances off-loading colour now
into angles as

I hang their weather in
your room, all the time wondering

just how I look from the road –
my blouse off-white and

my skirt the colour of
all the disappointments of a day when

the curtains are pulled back on
a dull morning.

Ghost Stories

Our American Hallowe'en was years ago. We wore
anoraks and gloves
and stood outside to watch

the moon above Iowa. Before dark,
I walked out

through the parking lot and playground
to our apartment block.

On every porch, every doorstep, candles fluttered in
pumpkins in the dusk on the eve
of the holiday. We

were strangers
there. I remember how our lighted rooms
looked through curtains from the road:

with that fragility.

What Love Intended

I can imagine if,
I came back again,
    looking through windows at

    broken mirrors, pictures,
and, in the cracked upstairs,
    the beds where it all began.

The suburb in the rain
this October morning,
    full of food and children

    and animals, will be –
when I come back again –
    gone to rack and ruin.

I will be its ghost,
its revenant, discovering
    again in one place

    the history of my pain,
my ordeal, my grace,
    unable to resist

seeing what is past,
judging what has ended
and whether, first to last,

from then to now and even
here, ruined, this
is what love intended –

finding even the yellow
jasmine in the dusk,
the smell of early dinners,

the voices of our children,
taking turns and quarrelling,
burned on the distance,

gone. And the small square
where under cropped lime
and poplar, on bicycles

and skates in the summer,
they played until dark;
propitiating time.

And even the two whitebeams
outside the house gone, with
the next-door-neighbour

who used to say in April –
when one was slow to bloom –
they were a man and woman.

Distances

The radio is playing downstairs in the kitchen.
The clock says eight and the light says
winter. You are pulling up your hood against a bad morning.

Don't leave, I say. Don't go without telling me
the name of that song. You call it back to me from the stairs –
'I Wish I Was In Carrickfergus'

and the words open out with emigrant grief the way the streets
of a small town open out in
memory: salt-loving fuchsias to one side and

a market in full swing on the other with
linen for sale and tacky apples and a glass and wire hill
of spectacles on a metal tray. The front door bangs

and you're gone. I will think of it all morning while a fine
drizzle closes in, making the distances
fiction: not of that place but this and of how

restless we would be, you and I, inside the perfect
music of that basalt and sandstone
coastal town. We would walk the streets in

the scentless afternoon of a ballad measure,
longing to be able
to tell each other that the starched lace and linen of

adult handkerchiefs scraped your face and left your tears
falling; how the apples were mush inside the crisp sugar
shell and the spectacles out of focus.

IN A TIME OF VIOLENCE
1994

The Singers

for M.R.

The women who were singers in the West
lived on an unforgiving coast.
I want to ask was there ever one
moment when all of it relented,
when rain and ocean and their own
sense of home were revealed to them
as one and the same?
                After which
every day was still shaped by weather,
but every night their mouths filled with
Atlantic storms and clouded-over stars
and exhausted birds.
            And only when the danger
was plain in the music could you know
their true measure of rejoicing in

finding a voice where they found a vision.

I Writing in a Time of Violence
A sequence

As in a city where the evil are permitted to have authority and the good are put out of the way, so in the soul of man, as we maintain, the imitative poet implants an evil constitution, for he indulges the irrational nature which has no discernment of greater or less.

Plato, The Republic: *X*

1 *That the Science of Cartography is Limited*

– and not simply by the fact that this shading of
forest cannot show the fragrance of balsam,
the gloom of cypresses
is what I wish to prove.

When you and I were first in love we drove
to the borders of Connacht
and entered a wood there.

Look down you said: this was once a famine road.

I looked down at ivy and the scutch grass
rough-cast stone had
disappeared into as you told me
in the second winter of their ordeal, in

1847, when the crop had failed twice,
Relief Committees gave
the starving Irish such roads to build.

Where they died, there the road ended

and ends still and when I take down
the map of this island, it is never so
I can say here is
the masterful, the apt rendering of

the spherical as flat, nor
an ingenious design which persuades a curve
into a plane,
but to tell myself again that

the line which says woodland and cries hunger
and gives out among sweet pine and cypress,
and finds no horizon

will not be there.

2   The Death of Reason

When the Peep-O-Day Boys were laying fires down in
the hayricks and seed-barns of a darkening Ireland,
the art of portrait-painting reached its height
across the water.
The fire caught.
The flames cracked and the light showed up the scaffold
and the wind carried staves of a ballad.
The flesh-smell of hatred.
And she climbed the stairs.
Nameless composite. Anonymous beauty-bait for the painter.
Rustling gun-coloured silks. To set a seal on Augustan London.
And sat down.
The easel waits for her
and the age is ready to resemble her and
the small breeze cannot touch that powdered hair.
That elegance.
But I smell fire.
From Antrim to the Boyne the sky is reddening as
the painter tints alizerine crimson with a mite of yellow
mixed once with white and finds out
how difficult it is to make the skin
blush outside the skin.
The flames have crossed the sea.
They are at the lintel. At the door.
At the canvas,

at her mouth.
And the curve and pout
of supple dancing and the couplet rhyming
and the pomander scenting death-rooms and
the cabinet-maker setting his veneers
in honest wood – they are kindling for the flames.
And the dictates of reason and the blended sensibility
of tact and proportion – yes
the eighteenth century ends here
as her hem scorches and the satin
decoration catches fire. She is burning down.
As a house might. As a candle will.
She is ash and tallow. It is over.

3   March 1 1847. By the First Post

The daffodils are out & how
you would love the harebells by
the Blackwater now.
But Etty, you are wise to stay away.
London may be dull in this season.
Meath is no better I assure you.
Your copper silk is sewn
& will be sent & I envy you.
No one talks of anything but famine.
I go nowhere –
not from door to carriage – but a cloth
sprinkled with bay rum & rose attar
is pressed against my mouth.
Our picnics by the river –
remember that one with Major Harris? –
our outings to the opera
& our teas
are over now for the time being.
Shall I tell you what I saw on Friday,
driving with Mama? A woman lying
across the Kells Road with her baby –
in full view. We had to go

out of our way
to get home & we were late
& poor Mama was not herself all day.

4 In a Bad Light

This is St Louis. Where the rivers meet.
The Illinois. The Mississippi. The Missouri.
The light is in its element of autumn.
Clear. With yellow gingko leaves falling.
There is always a nightmare. Even in such light.

The weather must be cold now in Dublin.
And when skies are clear frosts come
down on the mountains and the first
inklings of winter will be underfoot in
the crisp iron of a fern at dawn.

I stand in a room in the Museum.
In one glass case a plastic figure
represents a woman in a dress,
with crêpe sleeves and a satin apron.
And feet laced neatly into suede.

She stands in a replica of a cabin
on a steamboat bound for New Orleans.
The year is 1860. Nearly war.
A notice says no comforts were spared. The silk
is French. The seamstresses are Irish.

I see them in the oil-lit parlours.
I am in the gas-lit backrooms.
We make in the apron front and from
the papery appearance and crushable
look of crêpe, a sign. We are bent over

in a bad light. We are sewing a last
sight of shore. We are sewing coffin ships.
    And the salt of exile. And our own
death in it. For history's abandonment
    we are doing this. And this. And

this is a button hole. This is a stitch.
    Fury enters them the way frost follows
every arabesque and curl of a fern: this is
    the nightmare. See how you perceive it.
We sleep the sleep of exhaustion.

    We dream a woman on a steamboat
parading in sunshine in a dress we know
    we made. She laughs off rumours of war.
She turns and traps light on the skirt.
    It is, for that moment, beautiful.

5 The Dolls Museum in Dublin

The wounds are terrible. The paint is old.
The cracks along the lips and on the cheeks
cannot be fixed. The cotton lawn is soiled.
The arms are ivory dissolved to wax.

Recall the quadrille. Hum the waltz.
Promenade on the yacht-club terraces.
Put back the lamps in their copper holders,
the carriage wheels on the cobbled quays.

And recreate Easter in Dublin.
Booted officers. Their mistresses.
Sunlight criss-crossing College Green.
Steam hissing from the flanks of horses.

Here they are. Cradled and cleaned,
held close in the arms of their owners.
Their cold hands clasped by warm hands,
their faces memorised like perfect manners.

The altars are mannerly with linen.
The lilies are whiter than surplices.
The candles are burning and warning:
Rejoice, they whisper. After sacrifice.

Horse chestnuts hold up their candles.
The Green is vivid with parasols.
Sunlight is pastel and windless.
The bar of the Shelbourne is full.

Laughter and gossip on the terraces.
Rumour and alarm at the barracks.
The Empire is summoning its officers.
The carriages are turning: they are turning back.

Past children walking with governesses,
Looking down, cossetting their dolls,
then looking up as the carriage passes,
the shadow chilling them. Twilight falls.

It is twilight in the dolls museum. Shadows
remain on the parchment-coloured waists,
are bruises on the stitched cotton clothes,
are hidden in the dimples on the wrists.

The eyes are wide. They cannot address
the helplessness which has lingered in
the airless peace of each glass case:
to have survived. To have been stronger than

a moment. To be the hostages ignorance
takes from time and ornament from destiny. Both.
To be the present of the past. To infer the difference
with a terrible stare. But not feel it. And not know it.

6 Inscriptions

About holiday rooms there can be
a solid feel at first. Then, as you go upstairs,
the air gets
a dry rustle of excitement

the way a new dress comes out of tissue paper,
up and out of it, and
the girl watching this thinks:
Where will I wear it? Who will kiss me in it?

Peter
was the name on the cot.
The cot was made of the carefully bought
scarcities of the nineteen-forties:
oak. Tersely planed and varnished.
Cast-steel hinges.

I stood where the roof sloped into
paper roses,
in a room where a child once went to sleep,
looking at blue, painted lettering:

as he slept
someone had found for him
five pieces of the alphabet which said
the mauve petals of his eyelids as they closed out
the scalded hallway moonlight made of the ocean at
the end of his road.

Someone knew
the importance of giving him a name.

For years I have known
how important it is
not to name
the coffins, the murdered in them,
the deaths in alleyways and on doorsteps —

in case they rise out of their names
and I recognise

the child who slept peacefully
and the girl who guessed at her future in
the dress as it came out of its box
falling free in
kick pleats of silk.

And what comfort can there be
in knowing that
in a distant room
his sign is safe tonight
and reposes its modest blues in darkness?

Or that outside his window
the name-eating elements – the salt wind, the rain –
must find
headstones to feed their hunger?

7 Beautiful Speech

In my last year in College
I set out
to write an essay on
the Art of Rhetoric. I had yet to find

the country already lost to me
in song and figure as I scribbled down
names for sweet euphony
and safe digression.

And when I came to the word *insinuate*
I saw that language could writhe and creep
and the lore of snakes
which I had learned as a child not to fear –
because the Saint had sent them out of Ireland –
came nearer.

Chiasmus. Litotes. Periphrasis. Old
indices and agents of persuasion. How
I remember them in that room where
a girl is writing at a desk with
dusk already in
the streets outside. I can see her. I could say to her –

we will live, we have lived
where language is concealed. Is perilous.
We will be – we have been – citizens
of its hiding place. But it is too late

to shut the book of satin phrases,
to refuse to enter
an evening bitter with peat smoke,
where newspaper sellers shout headlines
and friends call out their farewells in
a city of whispers
and interiors where

the dear vowels
Irish Ireland ours are
absorbed into autumn air,
are out of earshot in the distances
we are stepping into where we never

imagine words such as *hate*
and *territory* and the like – unbanished still
as they always would be – wait
and are waiting under
beautiful speech. To strike.

II Legends

This Moment

A neighbourhood.
At dusk.

Things are getting ready
to happen
out of sight.

Stars and moths.
And rinds slanting around fruit.

But not yet.

One tree is black.
One window is yellow as butter.

A woman leans down to catch a child
who has run into her arms
this moment.

Stars rise.
Moths flutter.
Apples sweeten in the dark.

Love

Dark falls on this mid-western town
where we once lived when myths collided.
Dusk has hidden the bridge in the river
which slides and deepens
to become the water
the hero crossed on his way to hell.

Not far from here is our old apartment.
We had a kitchen and an Amish table.
We had a view. And we discovered there
love had the feather and muscle of wings
and had come to live with us,
a brother of fire and air.

We had two infant children one of whom
was touched by death in this town
and spared: and when the hero
was hailed by his comrades in hell
their mouths opened and their voices failed and
there is no knowing what they would have asked
about a life they had shared and lost.

I am your wife.
It was years ago.
Our child is healed. We love each other still.
Across our day-to-day and ordinary distances
we speak plainly. We hear each other clearly.

And yet I want to return to you
on the bridge of the Iowa river as you were,
with snow on the shoulders of your coat
and a car passing with its headlights on:

I see you as a hero in a text –
the image blazing and the edges gilded –
and I long to cry out the epic question
my dear companion:

Will we ever live so intensely again?
Will love come to us again and be
so formidable at rest it offered us ascension
even to look at him?

But the words are shadows and you cannot hear me.
You walk away and I cannot follow.

The Pomegranate

The only legend I have ever loved is
the story of a daughter lost in hell.
And found and rescued there.
Love and blackmail are the gist of it.
Ceres and Persephone the names.
And the best thing about the legend is
I can enter it anywhere. And have.
As a child in exile in
a city of fogs and strange consonants,
I read it first and at first I was
an exiled child in the crackling dusk of
the underworld, the stars blighted. Later
I walked out in a summer twilight
searching for my daughter at bed-time.
When she came running I was ready
to make any bargain to keep her.
I carried her back past whitebeams
and wasps and honey-scented buddleias.
But I was Ceres then and I knew
winter was in store for every leaf
on every tree on that road.
Was inescapable for each one we passed.
And for me.
                It is winter
and the stars are hidden.
I climb the stairs and stand where I can see
my child asleep beside her teen magazines,
her can of Coke, her plate of uncut fruit.
The pomegranate! How did I forget it?
She could have come home and been safe
and ended the story and all
our heart-broken searching but she reached
out a hand and plucked a pomegranate.
She put out her hand and pulled down
the French sound for apple and
the noise of stone and the proof
that even in the place of death,
at the heart of legend, in the midst
of rocks full of unshed tears

ready to be diamonds by the time
the story was told, a child can be
hungry. I could warn her. There is still a chance.
The rain is cold. The road is flint-coloured.
The suburb has cars and cable television.
The veiled stars are above ground.
It is another world. But what else
can a mother give her daughter but such
beautiful rifts in time?
If I defer the grief I will diminish the gift.
The legend will be hers as well as mine.
She will enter it. As I have.
She will wake up. She will hold
the papery flushed skin in her hand.
And to her lips. I will say nothing.

At the Glass Factory in Cavan Town

Today it is a swan:
            the guide tells us
these are in demand.
            The glass is made

of red lead and potash
            and the smashed bits
of crystal sinews
            and decanter stoppers

crated over there –
            she points – and shattered
on the stone wheel
            rimmed with emery.

Aromas of stone and
            fire. Deranged singing
from the grindstone.
            And behind that

a mirror – my
daughters' heads turned
away in it – garnering
grindstone and fire.

The glass blower goes
to the furnace.
He takes a pole
from the earth's

core: the earth's core
is remembered in
the molten globe at
the end of it.

He shakes the pole
carefully to and fro.
He blows once. Twice.
His cheeks puff and

puff up: he is
a cherub at the very
edge of a cornice with
a mouthful of zephyrs –

sweet intrusions into
leaves and lace hems.
And now he lays
the rod on its spindle.

It is red. It is
ruddy and cooler.
It is cool now
and as clear as

the distances of this
county with its drumlins,
its herons, its closed–
in waterways on which

we saw this morning
        as we drove over
here, a mated pair
        of swans. Such

blind grace as they
        floated with told us
they did not know
        that every hour

every day, and
        not far away from
there they were
        entering the legend of

themselves. They gave no
        sign of it. But what
caught my eye, my
        attention was the safety

they assumed as
        they sailed their own
images. Here, now –
        and knowing that

the mirror still holds
        my actual flesh –
I could say to them:
        reflection is the first

myth of loss, but
        they floated away and
away from me as if
        no one would ever blow

false airs on them
        or try their sinews
in the fire, at
        the core, and they

took no care
              not to splinter, they
showed no fear
              they would end as

this one which is
              uncut yet still might:
a substance of its own
              future form, both

fraction and refraction
              in the deal–wood
crate at the door
              we will leave by.

The Water-Clock

Thinking of ageing on a summer day
              of rain and more rain
I took a book down from a shelf
              and stopped to read
and found myself –
              how did it happen? –
              reflecting on
the absurd creation of the water-clock.
              Drops collected
on the bell-tongues of fuchsia
              outside my window.
                    Apple-trees
              dripped. I read about
the clepsydra: invention of an ancient world,
              which reconciled
                    element to argument
       before the alphabet
              had crossed the Hellespont.
                    Water dripped
       from above
       and turned a wheel

which was about to turn
a dial when I looked up and saw
the rain had stopped.
How could they have? I thought.
Taken an element, that is.
Which swallowed faces, stars, irises, Narcissus.
And posed as frost, ice, snow.
And had a feel for
the theatre
and catastrophe of floods. And
in an August storm
could bring the moon to heel.
And reduced it
to this? And the sun came out and
the afternoon cleared.
And in half an hour –
maybe even less –
every trace of rain had disappeared.

Moths

Tonight the air smells of cut grass.
Apples rust on the branches. Already summer is
a place mislaid between expectation and memory.

This has been a summer of moths.
Their moment of truth comes well after dark.
Then they reveal themselves at our window-
ledges and sills as a pinpoint. A glimmer.

The books I look up about them are full of legends:
ghost-swift moths with their dancing assemblies at dusk.
Their courtship swarms. How some kinds may steer by the moon.

The moon is up. The back windows are wide open.
Mid-July light fills the neighbourhood. I stand by the hedge.

Once again they are near the windowsill –
fluttering past the fuchsia and the lavender,
which is knee-high, and too blue to warn them

they will fall down without knowing how
or why what they steered by became, suddenly,
what they crackled and burned around. They will perish –

I am perishing – on the edge and at the threshold of
the moment all nature fears and tends towards:

the stealing of the light. Ingenious facsimile.

And the kitchen bulb which beckons them makes
my child's shadow longer than my own.

A Sparrow Hawk in the Suburbs

At that time of year there is a turn in the road where
the hermit tones and meadow colours of
two seasons heal into
one another.

When the wild ladder of a winter scarf is stored away in
a drawer eased by candle-grease and lemon balm
is shaken out from
the linen press.

Those are afternoons when the Dublin hills are so close,
so mauve and blue, we can be certain dark
will bring rain and
it does to

the borrowed shears and the love-seat in the garden where
a sparrow hawk was seen through the opal
white of apple trees
after Easter. And

I want to know how it happened that those days of bloom when
rumours of wings and sightings – always seen by
someone else, somewhere else –
filled the air,

together with a citrus drizzle of petals and clematis opening,
and shadows waiting on a gradual lengthening
in the light our children
stayed up

later by, over pages of wolves and dragons and learned to
measure the sanctuary of darkness by a small
danger – how and why
they have chilled

into these April nights I lie awake listening for wings I will
never see above the cold frames and
last frosts of our
back gardens.

In Which the Ancient History I Learn Is Not My Own

The linen map
hung from the wall.
The linen was shiny
and cracked in places.
The cracks were darkened by grime.
It was fastened to the classroom wall with
a wooden batten on
a triangle of knotted cotton.

The colours
were faded out
so the red of Empire –
the stain of absolute possession –
the mark once made from Kashmir
to the oast-barns of the Kent
coast south of us was
underwater coral.

Ireland was far away
and farther away
every year.
I was nearly an English child.
I could list the English kings.
I could name the famous battles.
I was learning to recognise
God's grace in history.

And the waters
of the Irish sea,
their shallow weave
and cross-grained blue green
had drained away
to the pale gaze
of a doll's china eyes –
a stare without recognition or memory.

We have no oracles,
no rocks or olive trees,
no sacred path to the temple
and no priestesses.
The teacher's voice had a London accent.
This was London. 1952.
It was Ancient History Class.
She put the tip

of the wooden
pointer on the map.
She tapped over ridges and dried-
out rivers and cities buried in
the sea and sea-scapes which
had once been land.
And stopped.
Remember this, children.

The Roman Empire was
the greatest Empire
ever known –
until our time of course –
while the Delphic Oracle
was reckoned to be
the exact centre
of the earth.

Suddenly
I wanted
to stand in front of it.
I wanted to trace over
and over the weave of my own country.
To read out names
I was close to forgetting.
Wicklow. Kilruddery. Dublin.

To ask
where exactly
was my old house?
Its brass One and Seven.
Its flight of granite steps.
Its lilac tree whose scent
stayed under your fingernails
for days.

For days –
she was saying – *even months,*
the ancients travelled
to the Oracle.
They brought sheep and killed them.
They brought questions about tillage and war.
They rarely left with more
than an ambiguous answer.

The Huguenot Graveyard at the Heart of the City

It is the immodesty we bring to these
names which have eased into ours, and
their graves in the alcove of twilight,
which shadows their exile.

There is a flattery in being a destination.
There is a vanity in being the last resort.
They fled the Edict of Nantes –
hiding their shadows on the roads from France –

and now under brambles and granite
faith lies low with the lives it
dispossessed, and the hands it emptied out,
and the sombre dances they were joined in.

The buses turn right at Stephen's Green.
Car exhausts and sirens fill the air. See
the planted wildness of their rest and
grant to them the least love asks of

the living. Say: *they had another life once.*
And think of them as they first heard of us:
huddled around candles and words failing as
the stubborn tongue of the South put

oo and *an* to the sounds of Dublin,
and of their silver fingers at the window-sill
in the full moon as they leaned out
to breathe the sweet air of Nîmes

for the last time, and the flame
burned down in a dawn agreed upon
for their heart-broken leave-taking. And,
for their sakes, accept in that moment,

this city with its colours of sky and day –
and which is dear to us and particular –
was not a place to them: merely
the one witty step ahead of hate which

is all that they could keep. Or stay.

The Parcel

There are dying arts and
one of them is
the way my mother used to make up a parcel.
Paper first. Mid-brown and coarse-grained as wood.
The worst sort for covering a Latin book neatly
or laying flat at Christmas on a pudding bowl.
It was a big cylinder. She snipped it open
and it unrolled quickly across the floor.
All business, all distance.
Then the scissors.
Not a glittering let-up but a dour
pair, black thumb-holes,
the shears themselves the colour of the rained-
on steps a man with a grindstone climbed up
in the season of lilac and snapdragon
and stood there arguing the rate for
sharpening the lawnmower and the garden pair
and this one. All-in.
The ball of twine was coarsely braided
and only a shade less yellow than
the flame she held under the blunt
end of the sealing-wax until
it melted and spread into a brittle
terracotta medal.
Her hair dishevelled, her tongue between her teeth,
she wrote the address in the quarters
twine had divided the surface into.
Names and places. Crayon and fountain-pen.
The town underlined once. The country twice.
It's ready for the post
she would say and if we want to know
where it went to –
a craft lost before we missed it – watch it go
into the burlap sack for collection.
See it disappear. Say
this is how it died
out: among doomed steamships and out-dated trains,
the tracks for them disappearing before our eyes,
next to station names we can't remember

on a continent we no longer
recognise. The sealing-wax cracking.
The twine unravelling. The destination illegible.

Lava Cameo

a brooch carved on volcanic rock

I like this story —

My grandfather was a sea-captain.
My grandmother always met him when his ship docked.
She feared the women at the ports —

except that it is not a story,
more a rumour or a folk memory,
something thrown out once in a random conversation;
a hint merely.

If I say wool and lace for her skirt and
crêpe for her blouse
in the neck of which is pinned a cameo,
carved out of black, volcanic rock;

if I make her pace the Cork docks, stopping
to take down her parasol as a gust catches
the silk tassels of it —

then consider this:

there is a way of making free with the past,
a pastiche of what is
real and what is
not, which can only be
justified if you think of it

not as sculpture but syntax:

a structure extrinsic to meaning which uncovers
the inner secret of it.

She will die at thirty-one in a fever ward.
He will drown nine years later in the Bay of Biscay.
They will never even be
sepia, and so I put down

the gangplank now between the ship and the ground.
In the story, late afternoon has become evening.
They kiss once, their hands touch briefly.
Please.

Look at me, I want to say to her: show me
the obduracy of an art which can
arrest a profile in the flux of hell.

Inscribe catastrophe.

The Source

The adults stood
making sounds of disappointment.

We were high up in the Wicklow hills,
in a circle of whins and lilacs.

We were looking for the source of a river.
We never found it.

Instead, we drove to its northern edge.
And there the river leaned into the afternoon –
all light, all intrusion –
the way a mirror interrupts a room.

See me kneeling in a room
whose boundary
is fog and the dusk of a strange city.

The mirror shows a child in bad light.

From the inlaid box I lift up something
closed in tissue-paper.
My mother's hair. A whole coil of it –
it is the colour of corn harvested in darkness.

As the light goes,
I hold in my hand the coarse weight and
hopeless safe-keeping

and there comes back to me
the adult language for mystery:

Maybe. Nearly. It could almost be.

Legends

for Eavan Frances

Tryers of firesides,
twilights. There are no tears in these.

Instead, they begin the world again,
making the mountain ridges blue
and the rivers clear and the hero fearless –

and the outcome always undecided
so the next teller can say *begin* and
again and astonish children.

Our children are our legends.
You are mine. You have my name.
My hair was once like yours.

And the world
is less bitter to me
because you will re-tell the story.

III Anna Liffey

Anna Liffey

Life, the story goes,
Was the daughter of Cannan,
And came to the plain of Kildare.
She loved the flat-lands and the ditches
And the unreachable horizon.
She asked that it be named for her.
The river took its name from the land.
The land took its name from a woman.

A woman in the doorway of a house.
A river in the city of her birth.

There, in the hills above my house,
The river Liffey rises, is a source.
It rises in rush and ling heather and
Black peat and bracken and strengthens
To claim the city it narrated.
Swans. Steep falls. Small towns.
The smudged air and bridges of Dublin.

Dusk is coming.
Rain is moving east from the hills.

If I could see myself
I would see
A woman in a doorway
Wearing the colours that go with red hair.
Although my hair is no longer red.

I praise
The gifts of the river.
Its shiftless and glittering
Re-telling of a city,
Its clarity as it flows,
In the company of runt flowers and herons,
Around a bend at Islandbridge
And under thirteen bridges to the sea.
Its patience at twilight –
Swans nesting by it,
Neon wincing into it.

Maker of
Places, remembrances,
Narrate such fragments for me:

One body. One spirit.
One place. One name.
The city where I was born.
The river that runs through it.
The nation which eludes me.

Fractions of a life
It has taken me a lifetime
To claim.

I came here in a cold winter.

I had no children. No country.
I did not know the name for my own life.

My country took hold of me.
My children were born.

I walked out in a summer dusk
To call them in.

One name. Then the other one.
The beautiful vowels sounding out home.

Make of a nation what you will
Make of the past
What you can –

There is now
A woman in a doorway.

It has taken me
All my strength to do this.

Becoming a figure in a poem.

Usurping a name and a theme.

A river is not a woman.
    Although the names it finds,
        The history it makes
And suffers –
    The Viking blades beside it,
        The muskets of the Redcoats,
            The flames of the Four Courts
Blazing into it
    Are a sign.
            Any more than
A woman is a river,
    Although the course it takes,
        Through swans courting and distraught willows,

Its patience
   Which is also its powerlessness,
      From Callary to Islandbridge,
         And from source to mouth,
Is another one.
               And in my late forties
Past believing
   Love will heal
      What language fails to know
And needs to say –
   What the body means –
      I take this sign
And I make this mark:
      A woman in the doorway of her house.
         A river in the city of her birth.
The truth of a suffered life.
            The mouth of it.

The seabirds come in from the coast.
The city wisdom is they bring rain.
I watch them from my doorway.
I see them as arguments of origin –
Leaving a harsh force on the horizon
Only to find it
Slanting and falling elsewhere.

Which water –
The one they leave or the one they pronounce –
Remembers the other?

I am sure
The body of an ageing woman
Is a memory
And to find a language for it
Is as hard
As weeping and requiring
These birds to cry out as if they could
Recognise their element
Remembered and diminished in
A single tear.

An ageing woman
Finds no shelter in language.
She finds instead
Single words she once loved
Such as 'summer' and 'yellow'
And 'sexual' and 'ready'
Have suddenly become dwellings
For someone else –
Rooms and a roof under which someone else
Is welcome, not her. Tell me,
Anna Liffey,
Spirit of water,
Spirit of place,
How is it on this
Rainy autumn night
As the Irish sea takes
The names you made, the names
You bestowed, and gives you back
Only wordlessness?

Autumn rain is
Scattering and dripping
From car-ports
And clipped hedges.
The gutters are full.

When I came here
I had neither
Children nor country.
The trees were arms.
The hills were dreams.

I was free
To imagine a spirit
In the blues and greens,
The hills and fogs
Of a small city.

My children were born.
My country took hold of me.
A vision in a brick house.
Is it only love
That makes a place?

I feel it change.
My children are
Growing up, getting older.
My country holds on
To its own pain.

I turn off
The harsh yellow
Porch light and
Stand in the hall.
Where is home now?

Follow the rain
Out to the Dublin hills.
Let it become the river.
Let the spirit of place be
A lost soul again.

In the end
It will not matter
That I was a woman. I am sure of it.
The body is a source. Nothing more.
There is a time for it. There is a certainty
About the way it seeks its own dissolution.
Consider rivers.
They are always en route to
Their own nothingness. From the first moment
They are going home. And so
When language cannot do it for us,
Cannot make us know love will not diminish us,
There are these phrases
Of the ocean
To console us.

Particular and unafraid of their completion.
In the end
Everything that burdened and distinguished me
Will be lost in this:
I was a voice.

Story

Two lovers in an Irish wood at dusk
are hiding from an old and vengeful king.

The wood is full of sycamore and elder.
And set in that nowhere which is anywhere.

And let the woman be slender. As I was at twenty.
And red-haired. As I was until recently.

They cling together listening to his hounds
get nearer in the twilight and the spring

thickets fill with the sound of danger.
Blossoms are the colour of blood and capture.

We can be safe, they say. We can start
a rumour in the wood to reach the king –

that she has lost her youth. That her mouth is
cold. That this woman is growing older.

They do not know. They have no idea
how much of this: the ocean-coloured peace

of the dusk, and the way legend stresses it,
depend on her to be young and beautiful.

They start the rumour in the last light.
But the light changes. The distance shudders.

And suddenly what is happening is not
what happens to the lovers in the wood

or an angry king and his frantic hounds
and the tricks and kisses he has planned.

But what is whispering out of sycamores.
And over river-noise. And by-passes harebells

and blue air. And is overheard by the birds
which are the elements of logic in an early

spring. And is travelling to enter a suburb
at the foothills of the mountains in Dublin.

And a garden with jasmine and poplars. And
a table at which I am writing. I am writing

a woman out of legend. I am thinking
how new it is – this story. How hard it will be to tell.

Time and Violence

The evening was the same as any other.
I came out and stood on the step.
The suburb was closed in the weather

of an early spring and the shallow tips
and washed-out yellows of narcissi
resisted dusk. And crocuses and snowdrops.

I stood there and felt the melancholy
of growing older in such a season,
when all I could be certain of was simply

in this time of fragrance and refrain,
whatever else might flower before the fruit,
and be renewed, I would not. Not again.

A car splashed by in the twilight.
Peat smoke stayed in the windless
air overhead and I might have missed it:

a presence. Suddenly. In the very place
where I would stand in other dusks, and look
to pick out my child from the distance,

was a shepherdess, her smile cracked,
her arm injured from the mantelpieces
and pastorals where she posed with her crook.

Then I turned and saw in the spaces
of the night sky constellations appear,
one by one, over roof-tops and houses,

and Cassiopeia trapped: stabbed where
her thigh met her groin and her hand
her glittering wrist, with the pin-point of a star.

And by the road where rain made standing
pools of water underneath cherry trees,
and blossoms swam on their images,

was a mermaid with invented tresses,
her breasts printed with the salt of it and all
the desolation of the North Sea in her face.

I went nearer. They were disappearing.
Dusk had turned to night but in the air –
did I imagine it? – a voice was saying:

This is what language did to us. Here
is the wound, the silence, the wretchedness
of tides and hillsides and stars where

we languish in a grammar of sighs,
in the high-minded search for euphony,
in the midnight rhetoric of poesie.

We cannot sweat here. Our skin is icy.
We cannot breed here. Our wombs are empty.
Help us to escape youth and beauty.

Write us out of the poem. Make us human
in cadences of change and mortal pain
and words we can grow old and die in.

The Art of Grief

I saw a statue yesterday. A veiled woman.
Head and shoulders only. Up on a pedestal.
A veil of grief covering her whole face.
I stood there, caught by surprise, my
car keys getting warmer in one hand,
both of us women in our middle years,
but hers were fixed, set and finished in
a mutton-fat creaminess, a seamless flutter in
marble revealed by a sudden brightness
from the window behind me and other parts
were as dark as the shell of a swan mussel.

I saw my mother weep once. It was under
circumstances I can never, even now,
weave into or reveal by these cadences.
As I watched, and I was younger then,
I could see that weeping itself has no cadence.
It is unrhythmical, unpredictable and
the intake of breath one sob needs to
become another sob, so one tear can succeed
another, is unmusical: whoever the muse is
or was of weeping, she has put the sound of it
beyond the reach of metric–makers, music–makers.

I went up to her. At the well
of the throat where tears start,
there the artist must have started,
I was sure of it. From there upwards –
chin, lips, skin lines, eyelids – all
had been chiselled out with the veil in
the same, indivisible act of definition
which had silenced her. No sound. Not one.
No dissonance of grief in a small room on
a summer evening. Just a mineral grace
in which she had found a rhythm to weep by.

The rhythm of summer was unstoppable: a rapt
heat waited for the blackbird to say dusk
is coming, is about to be, will be able to
fold the ladysmock, cowslips and the grey
undertips of the mulberry leaves into that
translucence which is all darkness can be in
this season. The room was curtained, quiet.
We sat at right-angles. I knew the late
sun would never make the cinnamon-and-
chintz pansies on those armrests grow
more or perish there. And my mother wept.

An object of the images we make is
what we are and how we lean out and
over the perfect surface where
our features in water greet and save us.
No weeping there: only the element
claiming its emblem. A last wheat-coloured
brightness filled the room. She dried her tears.
She put one hand up to her throat and pulled,
between her thumb and forefinger, the rope
of light there. 'Did you know' she said
'some people say that pearls are tears?'

I could not ask her, she could not tell me
why something had once made her weep.
Had made her cover up her mouth and eyes
in the slow work of the moth fed on
white mulberry leaves. Had made her say:
from now on let daylight be black
and white and menial in-betweens and
let the distances be made of silk. My
distances were made of grit and the light
rain throws away in the hour between planets.
And rush-hour traffic. My keys were ready.

What she knew was gone and what I
wanted to know she had never known:
the moment her sorrow entered marble –
the exact angle of the cut at which
the sculptor made the medium remember
its own ordeal in the earth, the aeons
crushing and instructing it until it wept itself
into inches, atoms of change. Above all,
whether she flinched as the chisel found
that region her tears inferred,
where grief and its emblems are inseparable.

A Woman Painted on a Leaf

I found it among curios and silver,
in the pureness of wintry light.

A woman painted on a leaf.

Fine lines drawn on a veined surface
in a hand-made frame.

This is not my face. Neither did I draw it.

A leaf falls in a garden.
The moon cools its aftermath of sap.
The pith of summer dries out in starlight.

A woman is inscribed there.

This is not death. It is the terrible
suspension of life.

I want a poem
I can grow old in. I want a poem I can die in.

I want to take
this dried-out face,
as you take a starling from behind iron,
and return it to its element of air, of ending –

so that autumn
which was once
the hard look of stars,
the frown on a gardener's face,
a gradual bronzing of the distance,

will be,
from now on,
a crisp tinder underfoot. Cheekbones. Eyes. Will be
a mouth crying out. Let me.

Let me die.

THE LOST LAND
1998

FOR MARY ROBINSON –
WHO FOUND IT

I Colony

1 My Country in Darkness

After the wolves and before the elms
the Bardic Order ended in Ireland.

Only a few remained to continue
a dead art in a dying land:

This is a man
on the road from Youghal to Cahirmoyle.
He has no comfort, no food and no future.
He has no fire to recite his friendless measures by.
His riddles and flatteries will have no reward.
His patrons sheath their swords in Flanders and Madrid.

Reader of poems, lover of poetry –
in case you thought this was a gentle art,
follow this man on a moonless night
to the wretched bed he will have to make:

The Gaelic world stretches out under a hawthorn tree
and burns in the rain. This is its home,
its last frail shelter. All of it –
Limerick, the Wild Geese and what went before –
falters into cadence before he sleeps:

He shuts his eyes. Darkness falls on it.

2 The Harbour

This harbour was made by art and force.
And called Kingstown and afterwards Dun Laoghaire.
And holds the sea behind its barrier
less than five miles from my house.

Lord be with us say the makers of a nation.
Lord look down say the builders of a harbour.
They came and cut a shape out of ocean
and left stone to close around their labour.

Officers and their wives promenaded
on this spot once and saw with their own eyes
the opulent horizon and obedient skies
which nine-tenths of the law provided.

And frigates with thirty-six guns cruising
the outer edges of influence could idle
and enter here and catch the tide of
empire and arrogance and the Irish sea rising

and rising through a century of storms
and cormorants and moonlight the whole length of this coast,
while an ocean forgot an empire and the armed
ships under it changed: to slime weed and cold salt and rust.

City of shadows and of the gradual
capitulations to the last invader
this is the final one: signed in water
and witnessed in granite and ugly bronze and gun-metal.

And by me. I am your citizen: composed of
your fictions, your compromise, I am
a part of your story and its outcome.
And ready to record its contradictions.

3 Witness

Here is the city –
its worn-down mountains,
its grass and iron,
its smoky coast
seen from the high roads
on the Wicklow side.

From Dalkey Island
to the North Wall,
to the blue distance seizing its perimeter,
its old divisions are deep within it.

And in me also.
And always will be:

Out of my mouth they come.
The spurred and booted garrisons.
The men and women
they dispossessed.

What is a colony
if not the brutal truth
that when we speak
the graves open.
And the dead walk?

4 Daughters of Colony

Daughters of parsons and of army men.
Daughters of younger sons of younger sons.
Who left for London from Kingstown harbour –
never certain which they belonged to.

Who took their journals and their steamer trunks.
Who took their sketching books.

Who wore hats
made out of local straw
dried in an Irish field beside a river which

flowed to a town they had known in childhood,
and watched forever from their bedroom windows,
framed in the clouds and cloud-shadows,
the blotchy cattle and

the scattered window lamps of a flat landscape
they could not enter.
Would never enter.

I see the darkness coming.
The absurd smallness of the handkerchiefs
they are waving
as the shore recedes.

I put my words between them
and the silence
the failing light has consigned them to:

I also am a daughter of the colony.
I share their broken speech, their other-whereness.

No testament or craft of mine can hide
our presence
on the distaff side of history.

See: they pull the brims of their hats
down against a gust from the harbour.

They cover
their faces with what should have been
and never quite was: their home.

5 Imago

Head of a woman. Half-life of a nation.
Coarsely-cut blackthorn walking stick.
Old Tara brooch.
And bog oak.
A harp and a wolfhound on an ashtray.

All my childhood
I took you for the truth.

I see you now for what you are.

My ruthless images. My simulacra.
Anti-art. A foul skill
traded by history
to show a colony

the way to make pain a souvenir.

6 The Scar

Dawn on the river.
Dublin rises out of what reflects it.

Anna Liffey
looks to the east, to the sea,
her profile carved out by the light
on the old Carlisle bridge.

I was five
when a piece of glass
cut my head and left a scar.
Afterwards my skin felt different.

And still does on these autumn days when
the mist hides the city
from the Liffey.

The Liffey hides
the long ships, the muskets and the burning domes.

Everything but this momentary place.
And those versions of the Irish rain
which change the features
of a granite face.

If colony is a wound what will heal it?
After such injuries
what difference do we feel?

No answer in the air,
on the water, in the distance.
And yet

Emblem of this old,
torn and traded city,
altered by its river, its weather,
I turn to you as if there were.

One flawed head towards another.

7 City of Shadows

When I saw my father
buttoning his coat at Front Gate
I thought he would look like a man
who had lost what he had. And he did.

Grafton Street and Nassau Street were gone.
And the old parliament at College Green.
And the bronze arms and attitudes of orators
from Grattan to O'Connell. All gone.

We went to his car. He got in.
I waved my hands and motioned him to turn
his wheel towards the road to the only
straight route out to the coast.

When he did
I walked beside the car,
beside the kerb, and we made our way
in dark inches to the Irish Sea.

Then I smelled salt
and heard the foghorn.
And realised suddenly that I
had brought my father to his destination.

I walked home
alone to my flat.
The fog was lifting slowly. I thought
whatever the dawn made clear

and cast-iron and adamant again,
I would know from now on that in
a lost land of orators and pedestals
and corners and street names and rivers,

where even the ground underfoot
was hidden from view, there had been
one way out.
And I found it.

8 Unheroic

It was an Irish summer. It was wet.
It was a job. I was seventeen.
I set the clock and caught the bus at eight
and leaned my head against the misty window.
The city passed by. I got off
above the Liffey on a street of statues:
iron orators and granite patriots.
Arms wide. Lips apart. Last words.

I worked in a hotel. I carried trays.
I carried keys. I saw the rooms
when they were used and airless and again
when they were aired and ready and I stood
above the road and stared down at
silent eloquence and wet umbrellas.

There was a man who lived in the hotel.
He was a manager. I rarely saw him.
There was a rumour that he had a wound
from war or illness – no one seemed sure –
which would not heal. And when he finished
his day of ledgers and telephones he went
up the back stairs to his room
to dress it. I never found out
where it was. Someone said in his thigh.
Someone else said deep in his side.

He was a quiet man. He spoke softly.
I saw him once or twice on the stairs
at the back of the building by the laundry.
Once I waited, curious to see him.

Mostly I went home. I got my coat
and walked bare-headed to the river
past the wet, bronze and unbroken skin
of those who learned their time and knew their country.

How do I know my country? Let me tell you
it has been hard to do. And when I do
go back to difficult knowledge, it is not
to that street or those men raised
high above the certainties they stood on –
Ireland hero history – but how

I went behind the linen room and up
the stone stairs and climbed to the top.
And stood for a moment there, concealed
by shadows. In a hiding place.
Waiting to see.
Wanting to look again.
Into the patient face of the unhealed.

9 The Colonists

I am ready to go home
through an autumn evening.

Suddenly,
without any warning, I can see them.

They form slowly out of the twilight.
Their faces. Arms. Greatcoats. And tears.

They are holding maps.
But the pages are made of failing daylight.
Their tears, made of dusk, fall across the names.

Although they know by heart
every inch and twist of the river
which runs through this town, and their houses –
every aspect of the light their windows found –
they cannot find where they come from:

The river is still there.
But not their town.
The light is there. But not their moment in it.
Nor their memories. Nor the signs of life they made.

Then they faded.
And the truth is I never saw them.
If I had I would have driven home
through an ordinary evening, knowing
that not one street name or sign or neighbourhood

could be trusted
to the safe-keeping
of the making and unmaking of a people.

And have entered a house I might never
find again, and have written down –
as I do now –

their human pain. Their ghostly weeping.

10 *A Dream of Colony*

I dreamed we came to an iron gate.
And leaned against it.

It opened.
We heard it grinding slowly over gravel.

We began to walk.
When we started talking
I saw our words had the rare power
to unmake history:

Gradually the elms beside us
shook themselves into leaves.
And laid out under us their undiseased shadows.

Each phrase of ours,
holding still for a moment in the stormy air,
raised an unburned house
at the end of an avenue of elder and willow.

Unturned that corner
the assassin eased around and aimed from.
Undid. Unsaid:
Once. Fire. Quick. Over there.

The scarred granite healed in my sleep.
The thundery air became sweet again.
We had come to the top of the avenue.

I heard laughter and forgotten consonants.
I saw greatcoats and epaulettes.
I turned to you –

but who are you?

Before I woke I heard a woman's voice cry out.
It was hoarse with doubt.
She was saying,
I was saying –

What have we done?

11 A Habitable Grief

Long ago
I was a child in a strange country:

I was Irish in England.

I learned
a second language there
which has stood me in good stead –

the lingua franca of a lost land.

A dialect in which
what had never been could still be found.

That infinite horizon. Always far
and impossible. That contrary passion
to be whole.

This is what language is:
a habitable grief. A turn of speech
for the everyday and ordinary abrasion
of losses such as this

which hurts
just enough to be a scar.

And heals just enough to be a nation.

12 The Mother Tongue

The old pale ditch can still be seen
less than half a mile from my house –

its ancient barrier of mud and brambles
which mireth next unto Irishmen
is now a mere rise of coarse grass,
a rowan tree and some thinned-out spruce,
where a child is playing at twilight.

I stand in the shadows. I find it
hard to believe now that once
this was a source of our division:

Dug. Drained. Shored up and left
to keep out and keep in. That here
the essence of a colony's defence
was the substance of the quarrel with its purpose:

Land. Ground. A line drawn in rain
and clay and the roots of wild broom –
behind it the makings of a city,
beyond it rumours of a nation –
by Dalkey and Kilternan and Balally
through two ways of saying their names.

A window is suddenly yellow.
A woman is calling a child.
She turns from her play and runs to her name.

Who came here under cover of darkness
from Glenmalure and the Wicklow hills
to the limits of this boundary? Who whispered
the old names for love to this earth
and anger and ownership as it opened
the abyss of their future at their feet?

I was born on this side of the Pale.
I speak with the forked tongue of colony.
But I stand in the first dark and frost
of a winter night in Dublin and imagine

my pure sound, my undivided speech
travelling to the edge of this silence.
As if to find me. And I listen: I hear
what I am safe from. What I have lost.

II   The Lost Land

for Jody Allen-Randolph

Home

Off a side road in southern California
is a grove of eucalyptus.
It looks as if
someone once came here with a handful

of shadows, not seeds, and planted them.
And they turned into trees.
But the leaves
have a tell-tale blueness and deepness.

Up a slope to the left is a creek.
Across it lies a cut-down tree trunk.
Further back again is the faraway,
filtered-out glitter of the Pacific.

I went there one morning with a friend
in mid-October
when the monarch butterflies
arrive from their westward migration –

thousands of them. Hundreds of thousands
collecting in a single location.

I climbed to the creek and looked up.
Every leaf was covered and ended in
a fluttering struggle.

Atmosphere. Ocean. Oxygen and dust
were altered by their purposes.
They had changed the trees to iron.
They were rust.

I looked at my watch. It was early.
But my mind was ready
for the evening
they were darkening into overhead.

Every inch and atom of daylight
was filled with their beating and flitting,
their rising and flying at the hour
when dusk falls on a coastal city

where I had my hands full of shadows.
Once. And planted them.
And they became
a suburb and a house and a doorway
entered by and open to an evening
every room was lighted to offset.

I once thought that a single word
had the power to change.
To transform.

But these had not been changed.
And I would not be changed by it again.

If I could not say the word *home*.
If I could not breathe the Irish night
air and inference of rain coming from the east,

I could at least be sure –
far below them and unmoved by movement –
of one house with its window, making

an oblong of wheat out of light.

The Lost Land

I have two daughters.

They are all I ever wanted from the earth.

Or almost all.

I also wanted one piece of ground.

One city trapped by hills. One urban river.
An island in its element.

So I could say *mine. My own.*
And mean it.

Now they are grown up and far away

and memory itself
has become an emigrant,
wandering in a place
where love dissembles itself as landscape.

Where the hills
are the colours of a child's eyes,
where my children are distances, horizons.

At night,
on the edge of sleep,
I can see the shore of Dublin Bay,
its rocky sweep and its granite pier.

Is this, I say
how they must have seen it,
backing out on the mailboat at twilight,

shadows falling
on everything they had to leave?
And would love forever?
And then

I imagine myself
at the landward rail of that boat
searching for the last sight of a hand.

I see myself
on the underworld side of that water,
the darkness coming in fast, saying
all the names I know for a lost land.

Ireland. Absence. Daughter.

Mother Ireland

At first
    I was land
        I lay on my back to be fields
and when I turned
    on my side
        I was a hill
under freezing stars.
    I did not see.
        I was seen,
Night and day
    words fell on me.
                Seeds. Raindrops.
Chips of frost.
    From one of them
        I learned my name.
                I rose up. I remembered it.
Now I could tell my story.
    It was different
        from the story told about me.
And now also
    it was spring.
        I could see the wound I had left
in the land by leaving it.
    I travelled west.
                Once there
    I looked with so much love
        at every field
as it unfolded

its rusted wheel and its pram chassis
and at the gorse-
bright distances
I had been
that they misunderstood me.
Come back to us
they said.
Trust me I whispered

The Blossom

A May morning.
Light starting in the sky.

I have come here
after a long night.
Its senses of loss.
Its unrelenting memories of happiness.

The blossom on the apple tree is still in shadow,
its petals half-white and filled with water at the core,
in which the freshness and secrecy of dawn are stored
even in the dark.

How much longer
will I see girlhood in my daughter?

In other seasons
I knew every leaf on this tree.
Now I stand here
almost without seeing them

and so lost in grief
I hardly notice what is happening
as the light increases and the blossom speaks,
and turns to me
with blonde hair and my eyebrows and says –

imagine if I stayed here,
even for the sake of your love,
what would happen to the summer?
To the fruit?

Then holds out a dawn-soaked hand to me,
whose fingers I counted at birth
years ago.

And touches mine for the last time.

And falls to earth.

Daughter

i. The Season

The edge of spring.
The dark is wet. Already
stars are tugging at
their fibrous roots.

In February
they will fall and shine
from the roadsides
in their yellow hundreds.

My first child
was conceived in this season.
If I wanted a child now
I could not have one.

Except through memory.
Which is the ghost of the body.
Or myth.
Which is the ghost of meaning.

ii. The Loss

All morning
the sound of chain-saws.
My poplar tree has been cut down.

In dark spring dawns
when I could hardly raise
my head from the pillow

its sap rose
thirty feet into the air.
Into daylight. Into the last of starlight.

I go out to the garden
to touch the hurt wood spirits.
The injured summers.

Out of one of them a child runs.
Her skin printed with leaf-shadow.

And will not look at me.

iii. The Bargain

The garden creaks with rain.
The gutters run with noisy water.
The earth shows its age and makes a promise
only myth can keep. *Summer. Daughter.*

Ceres Looks at the Morning

I wake slowly. Already
my body is a twilight. Solid. Cold.
At the edge of a larger darkness. But outside
my window
a summer day is beginning. Apple trees

appear, one by one. Light is pouring
into the promise of fruit.
                          Beautiful morning
look at me as a daughter would
look: with that love and that curiosity –
as to what she came from.
And what she will become.

Tree of Life

A tree on a moonless night
has no sap or colour.

It has no flower and no fruit.

It waits for the sun to find them.

I cannot find you
in this dark hour
dear child.

Wait
for dawn to make us clear to one another.

Let the sun
inch above the roof-tops,

Let love
be the light that shows again

the blossom to the root.

Commissioned by the National Maternity Hospital, Dublin, during its 1994
Centenary, to mark a service to commemorate the babies who had died there.

Escape

I

It was only when a swan
made her nest
on the verge beside Leeson Street bridge,

and too near the kerb by the canal,
that I remembered
my first attempt at an Irish legend.

And stopped the car
and walked over to her.
And into my twentieth winter:

II

The window open where I left it.
The table cloth still on the table.
The page at the last line I crafted.

III

I sat in the kitchen and frost
blended with kettle steam while
I crossed out and crossed out
the warm skin and huggable limbs
of Lir's children –
rhyming them into doomed swans
cursed into flight on
a coast that was only half a mile
from my flat in Morehampton Road.

IV

It was evening now. Overhead
wild stars had wheels and landing gear.

A small air of spring hung above
the verge with its bottle lids and papers,
its poplar shadows,
its opening narcissi
and passers-by hurrying home from offices,
who barely turned to see what was there:

V

A mother bird too near the road.

A middle-aged woman going
as near to her as she dared.

Neither of them willing
to stir from the actual and ordinary,
momentary danger.

One of them aware of the story.

Both of them escaped from the telling.

Dublin, 1959

The café had
plastic chairs and lunch counters.
Its doors opened out on O'Connell Street.

I hunched my knees
under the table. The vinegar bottle
shifted its bitter yellows.

Tell me a story about Ireland
I said as a child
to anyone in earshot: about what had been
left behind by a modern world.
But not by memory.

I remember
we paid for our tea with a single pound note.
And walked out. And a bicycle went by,
its bell ringing loudly. And a car swerved around it.

Watching Old Movies When They Were New

I grew up in grey and white,
in half-tones and undertones,
sitting by a Bakelite telephone,
watching grainy and snowy kisses on the small screen.
This was New York.
I was thirteen. Outside my window the gardenless
and flowerless city, with its sirens
its cents, was new to me. And I was tired
of being anywhere but home. So I settled back
to get older quickly.
And the crescent moon,
and the shirt-collar of that man
as he kissed the girl under it and her face
as she turned away and the ocean beginning
to burn and glisten in the distance:
They were like me: what they lacked was
outside them. Was an absence within which
they could only be
less than themselves. Anyone could see
their doom was not love, was not destiny, was only
monochrome. But a time was coming. Is coming. Has come
and gone. And I will know what I am watching is
a passionate economy
we call the past. Although
its other name may be memory. And somewhere else

the future is already growing consequences. They are blue
and yellow. They are vermilion or a vivid green.
Pick us, they will say. *Bring us indoors.*
Arrange us into a city.
Into a situation. See how quickly
you tire of us. How soon you will yearn
for these tones. But I know
nothing of this as I lean back. As the screen flickers.

Heroic

Sex and history. And skin and bone.
And the oppression of Sunday afternoon.
Bells called the faithful to devotion.

I was still at school and on my own.
And walked and walked and sheltered from the rain.

The patriot was made of drenched stone.
His lips were still speaking. The gun
he held had just killed someone.

I looked up. And looked at him again.
He stared past me without recognition.

I moved my lips and wondered how the rain
would taste if my tongue were made of stone.
And wished it was. And whispered so that no one
could hear it but him. *Make me a heroine.*

Happiness

A Connemara summer. 1940.
My father is learning Irish.
My mother
is painting the harvest.

She holds umber and burnt orange
up against the canvas.

He says
samradh for summer and *atais* for happiness.

The Atlantic
salts the dark. She packs her colours.

It is time to go home
to the city where I have yet to be born.

They cannot see my sadness as the train
moves east through fields, shadows, farms
towards my life.

They do not hear the wheels
saying – as I can –

never again, never again.

The Last Discipline

In the evening
after a whole day at the easel
my mother would put down her brush,
pour turpentine into a glass jar,
and walk to the table.

Then she took a mirror,
hand-sized, enamelled in green,
and turned her back to the canvas.
And stood there.
And looked in it.

It was dusk.
The sheets were ghostly.
The canvas was almost not there.
In the end all I could see was her hand
closed around the handle.

All I can see now
is her hand, her head.
Her back is turned to what she made.
The mirror shows her
what is over her shoulder:

A room in winter.
A window with fog outside it.
A painting she sees is not finished.
A child: her face round with impatience,
who will return,

who has returned,
who only knows now that she has seen
the rare and necessary —
usually unobservable —
last discipline.

The Proof that Plato Was Wrong

August. And already
  light is assembling
another season at
  the end of an avenue
of water every tree is
  getting ready to
shed its leaves under.
  I was young here.
I am older here.
  I have come here
to find courage in
  the way this dawn
reaches slowly down
  the canal and reveals
a drowned summer
  which is almost over.
In the submarine
  greenness of these trees
whose roots and sinews
  are only – after all –
rain. And in these birds
  which cannot be heard,
which will never be
  heard. But are still
beginning to
  raise their heads
and open out
  their flooded wings,
as if they had not
  forgotten what
song is.

The Necessity for Irony

On Sundays,
when the rain held off,
after lunch or later,
I would go with my twelve-year-old
daughter into town,
and put down the time
at junk sales, antique fairs.

There I would
lean over tables,
absorbed by
lace, wooden frames,
glass. My daughter stood
at the other end of the room,
her flame-coloured hair
obvious whenever –
which was not often –

I turned around.
I turned around.
She was gone.
Grown. No longer ready
to come with me, whenever
a dry Sunday
held out its promises
of small histories. Endings.

When I was young
I studied styles: their use
and origin. Which age
was known for which
ornament and was always drawn
to a lyric speech, a civil tone.
But never thought
I would have the need,
as I do now, for a darker one.

Spirit of irony,
my caustic author
of the past, of memory –
and of its pain, which returns
hurts, stings – reproach me now,
remind me
that I was in those rooms,
with my child,
with my back turned to her,
searching – oh irony! –
for beautiful things.

Formal Feeling

A winged god
came to a woman at night.

Eros you know the story. You ordained it.

The one condition was she did not see him.

So it was dark when he visited her bed.
And it was good. She felt how good it was.
But she was curious. And lit a lamp.
And saw his nakedness. And he fled.

Into the dark. Into the here and now
and air and quiet of an Irish night,
where I am writing at a darkening window
about a winged god and his lover,

watching the lines and stanzas and measures,
which were devised for these purposes,
disappearing as the shadows close
in around the page
under my hand.

How can I know a form unless I see it?
How can I see it now?

I propose
the light she raised over his sleeping body
angered heaven because it made clear
neither his maleness nor his birth, nor
his face dreaming, but

the place where the sinew of his wings
touched the heat of his skin
and flight was brought down –

To this. To us. To earth.

Eros look down.
See as a god sees
what a myth says: how a woman still
addresses the work of man in the dark of the night.

The power of a form. The plain
evidence that strength descended here once.
And mortal pain. And even sexual glory.

And see the difference.
This time – and this you did not ordain –
I am changing the story.

Whose?

Beautiful land the patriot said
and rinsed it with his blood. And the sun rose.
And the river burned. The earth leaned
towards him. Shadows grew long. Ran red.

Beautiful land I whispered. But the roads
stayed put. Stars froze over the suburb.
Shadows iced up. Nothing moved.
Except my hand across the page. And these words.

CODE

2001

FOR MY HUSBAND, KEVIN CASEY

I Marriage

I In Which Hester Bateman, Eighteenth-Century English Silversmith, Takes an Irish Commission

Hester Bateman made a marriage spoon
And then subjected it to violence.
Chased, beat it. Scarred it and marked it.
All in the spirit of our darkest century:

Far away from grapeshot and tar caps
And the hedge schools and the music of sedition
She is oblivious to she pours out
And lets cool the sweet colonial metal.

Here in miniature a man and woman
Emerge beside each other from the earth,
From the deep mine, from the seams of rock
Which made inevitable her craft of hurt.

They stand side by side on the handle.
She writes their names in the smooth
Mimicry of a lake the ladle is making, in
A flowing script with a moon drowned in it.

Art and marriage: now a made match.
The silver bends and shines and in its own
Mineral curve an age-old tension
Inches towards the light. See how

Past and future and the space between
The semblance of empire, the promise of nation,
Are vanishing in this mediation
Between oppression and love's remembrance

Until resistance is their only element. It is
What they embody, bound now and always.
History frowns on them, yet in its gaze
They join their injured hands and make their vows.

II Against Love Poetry

We were married in summer, thirty years ago. I have loved
you deeply from that moment to this. I have loved other things as
well. Among them the idea of women's freedom. Why do I put these
words side by side? Because I am a woman. Because marriage is not
freedom. Therefore, every word here is written against love poetry.
Love poetry can do no justice to this. Here, instead, is a remembered
story from a faraway history: A great king lost a war and was paraded
in chains through the city of his enemy. They taunted him. They
brought his wife and children to him – he showed no emotion. They
brought his former courtiers – he showed no emotion. They brought
his old servant – only then did he break down and weep. I did not find
my womanhood in the servitudes of custom. But I saw my humanity
look back at me there. It is to mark the contradictions of a daily love
that I have written this. Against love poetry.

III The Pinhole Camera

solar eclipse, August 1999

This is the day
    and in preparation
        you punch a hole
in a piece of card.
        You hold it up against
a sheet of paper –
        the simplest form
of a pinhole camera –

and put the sun
on your right shoulder.
A bright disc
appears on your page.
It loses half its diameter.
And more than half
in another minute.
You know
the reason for the red berries
darkening, and the road outside
darkening, but did you know
that the wedding
of light and gravity
is forever?
The sun is in eclipse:
if this were legend
the king of light would turn his face away.
A single shadow
would kill the salmon-rich
rivers and birdlife
and lilac of this island.
But this is real —
how your page records
the alignment of planets,
their governance.
In other words,
the not-to-be-seen-again
mystery of
a mutual influence.
The motorways
are flowing north.
The sycamores are a perfect green.
The wild jasmine
is a speaking white.
The sun is coming back. As
it will. As it must.
You track its progress.
I stand and watch.
For you and I
such science holds no secrets:
We are married thirty years,
woman and man.

Long enough
to know about power and nature.
Long enough
to know which is which.

IV *Quarantine*

In the worst hour of the worst season
of the worst year of a whole people
a man set out from the workhouse with his wife.
He was walking – they were both walking – north.

She was sick with famine fever and could not keep up.
He lifted her and put her on his back.
He walked like that west and west and north.
Until at nightfall under freezing stars they arrived.

In the morning they were both found dead.
Of cold. Of hunger. Of the toxins of a whole history.
But her feet were held against his breastbone.
The last heat of his flesh was his last gift to her.

Let no love poem ever come to this threshold.
There is no place here for the inexact
praise of the easy graces and sensuality of the body.
There is only time for this merciless inventory:

Their death together in the winter of 1847.
Also what they suffered. How they lived.
And what there is between a man and woman.
And in which darkness it can best be proved.

V Embers

One night in winter when a bitter frost
made the whin-paths crack underfoot,
a wretched woman, eyes staring, hair in disarray,
came to the place where the Fianna had pitched camp.

Your face is made of shadow. You are reading.
There is heat from the fire still. I am reading:

She asked every one of them in turn
to take her to his bed, to shelter her with his body.
Each one looked at her – she was old beyond her years.
Each one refused her, each spurned her, except Diarmuid.

When he woke in the morning she was young and beautiful.
And she was his, forever, but on one condition.
He could not say that she had once been old and haggard.
He could not say that she had ever ... here I look up.

You are turned away. You have no interest in this.

I made this fire from the first peat of winter.
Look at me in the last, burnished light of it.
Tell me that you feel the warmth still.
Tell me you will never speak about the ashes.

VI Then

Where are the lives we lived
when we were young?
Our kisses, the heat of our skin, our bitter words?
The first waking to the first child's cry?

VII First Year

It was our first home –
our damp, upstairs,
one-year eyrie –
above a tree-lined area
nearer the city.

My talkative, unsure,
unsettled self
was everywhere;
but you
were the clear spirit of somewhere.

At night
when we settled down
in the big bed by the window,
over the streetlight
and the first crackle of spring

eased the iron at
the base of the railings,
unpacking crocuses,
it was
the awkward corners of your snowy town

which filled
the rooms we made
and stayed there all year with
the burnt-orange lampshade,
the wasps in the attic.

Where is the soul of a marriage?

Because I am writing this
not to recall our lives,
but to imagine them,
I will say it is
in the first gifts of place:

the steep inclines
and country silences
of your boyhood,
the orange-faced narcissi
and the whole length of the Blackwater

strengthening our embrace.

VIII Once

The lovers in an Irish story never had good fortune.
They fled the king's anger. They lay on the forest floor.
They kissed at the edge of death.

Did you know our suburb was a forest?
Our roof was a home for thrushes.
Our front door was a wild shadow of spruce.

Our faces edged in mountain freshness,
we took our milk in where the wide apart
prints of the wild and never-seen
creatures were set who have long since died out.

I do not want us to be immortal or unlucky.
To listen for our own death in the distance.
Take my hand. Stand by the window.

I want to show you what is hidden in
this ordinary, ageing human love is
there still and will be until

an inland coast so densely wooded
not even the ocean fog could enter it
appears in front of us and the chilled-
to-the-bone light clears and shows us

Irish wolves. A silvery man and wife.
Yellow-eyed. Edged in dateless moonlight.
They are mated for life. They are legendary. They are safe.

IX Thankëd be Fortune

Did we live a double life?
        I would have said
                we never envied
the epic glory of the star-crossed.
        I would have said
                we learned by heart
the code marriage makes of passion –
                duty dailyness routine.
But after dark when we went to bed
under the bitter fire
                of constellations,
        orderly uninterested and cold –
                at least in our case –
in the bookshelves just above our heads,
        all through the hours of darkness,
                men and women
wept, cursed, kept and broke faith
        and killed themselves for love.
                Then it was dawn again.
Restored to ourselves,
        we woke early and lay together
listening to our child crying, as if to birdsong,
        with ice on the windowsills
                and the grass eking out
        the last crooked hour of starlight.

X A Marriage for the Millennium

Do you believe
that Progress is a woman?
A spirit seeking for its opposite?
For a true marriage to ease her quick heartbeat?

I asked you this
as you sat with your glass of red wine
and your newspaper of yesterday's events.
You were drinking and reading, and did not hear me.

Then I closed the door
and left the house behind me and began
driving the whole distance of our marriage,
away from the suburb towards the city.

One by one
the glowing windows went out.
Television screens cooled down more slowly.
Ceramic turned to glass, circuits to transistors.

Old rowans were saplings.
Roads were no longer wide.
Children disappeared from their beds.
Wives, without warning, suddenly became children.

Computer games became codes again.
The codes were folded
back into the futures of their makers.
Their makers woke from sleep, weeping for milk.

When I came to the street we once lived on
with its iron edges out of another century
I stayed there only a few minutes.
Then I was in the car, driving again.

I was ready to tell you when I got home
that high above that street in a room
above the laid-out hedges and wild lilac
nothing had changed

them, nothing ever would.
The man with his creased copy of the newspaper.
Or the young woman talking to him. Talking to him.
Her heart eased by this.

XI. Lines for a Thirtieth Wedding Anniversary

Somewhere up in the eaves it began.
High in the roof – in a sort of vault
between the slates and gutter – a small leak.
Through it, rain which came from the east,
in from the lights and foghorns of the coast,
water with a ghost of ocean salt in it,
spilled down on the path below.
Over and over and over
years stone began to alter,
its grain searched out, worn in:
granite rounding down, giving way
taking into its own inertia that
information water brought – of ships,
wings, fog and phosphor in the harbour.
It happened under our lives, the rain,
the stone. We hardly noticed. Now
this is the day to think of it, to wonder.
All those years, all those years together –
the stars in a frozen arc overhead,
the quick noise of a thaw in the air,
the blue stare of the hills – through it all
this constancy: what wears, what endures.

II Code

Limits

So high
in their leafy silence
over Kells, over Durrow
as the Vikings
raged south –
the old monks
made the alphabet
wild:
　　　they dipped iron
into azure and
indigo: they gave strange
wings to their o's
and e's: their vowels
clung on with
talons and the thin,
ribbed wolves
which had gone north
left their frozen winters
and were lured back
to their consonants.

Code

an ode to Grace Murray Hopper 1906–88
maker of a computer compiler and verifier of COBOL

Poet to poet. I imagine you
    at the edge of language, at the start of summer,
      in Wolfeboro New Hampshire, writing code.
        You have no sense of time. No sense of minutes even.
        They cannot reach inside your world,
          your grey workstation
            with *when yet now never* and *once*.
              You have missed the other seven.
                This is the eighth day of creation.

The peacock has been made, the rivers stocked.
The rainbow has leaned down to clothe the trout.
The earth has found its pole, the moon its tides.
Atoms, energies have done their work,
have made the world, have finished it, have rested.
And we call this Creation. And you missed it.

The line of my horizon, solid blue
    appears at last fifty years away
      from your fastidious, exact patience.
        The first sign that night will be day
          is a stir of leaves in this Dublin suburb
            and air and invertebrates and birds,
          as the earth resorts again
            to its explanations.
              Its shadows. Its reflections. Its words.

You are west of me and in the past.
Dark falls. Light is somewhere else.
The fireflies come out above the lake.
You are compiling binaries and zeroes.
The given world is what you can translate.
And you divide the lesser from the greater.

Let there be language –
even if we use it differently:
I never made it timeless as you have.
I never made it numerate as you did.
And yet I use it here to imagine
how at your desk in the twilight
legend, history and myth of course,
are gathering in Wolfeboro New Hampshire,
as if to a memory. As if to a source.

Maker of the future, if the past
is fading from our view with the light
outside your window and the single file
of elements and animals, and all the facts
of origin and outcome, which will never find
their way to you or shelter in your syntax –

it makes no difference to us.
We are still human. There is still light
in my suburb and you are in my mind –
head bowed, old enough to be my mother –
writing code before the daylight goes.
I am writing at a screen as blue
as any hill, as any lake, composing this
to show you how the world begins again.
One word at a time.
One woman to another.

Making Money

At the turn of the century, the paper produced there was of such high
quality that it was exported for use as bank-note paper.
                                            'Dundrum and its Environs'

They made money –
                              maybe not the way
you think it should be done
but they did it anyway.

At the end of summer
the rains came and braided
the river Slang as it ran down and down
the Dublin mountains and into faster water
and stiller air as if a storm was coming in.
And the mill wheel turned so the mill
could make paper and the paper money.
And the cottage doors opened and the women
came out in the ugly first hour
after dawn and began

                              to cook the rags they put
hemp waste, cotton lint, linen, flax and fishnets
from boxes delivered every day on
the rag wagon on a rolling boil. And the steam rose
up from the open coils where a shoal slipped through
in an April dawn. And in the backwash they added
alkaline and caustic and soda ash and suddenly
they were making money.

                    A hundred years ago
this is the way they came to the plum-brown
headlong weir and the sedge drowned in it
and their faces about to be as they looked down
once quickly on
their way to the mill, to the toil
of sifting and beating and settling and fraying
the weighed-out fibres. And they see how easily
the hemp has forgotten the Irish sea at
neap tide and how smooth the weave is now in
their hands. And they do not and they never will

see the small boundaries all this will buy
or the poisoned kingdom with its waterways
and splintered locks or the peacocks who will walk
this paper up and down in the windless gardens
of a history no one can stop happening now.
Nor the crimson and indigo features
of the prince who will stare out from
the surfaces they have made on
the ruin of a Europe
he cannot see from the surface
of a wealth he cannot keep
                        if you can keep
your composure in the face of this final proof that
the past is not made out of time, out of memory,
out of irony but is also
a crime we cannot admit and will not atone
it will be dawn again in the rainy autumn of the year.
The air will be a skinful of water –
the distance between storms –
again. The wagon of rags will arrive.
The foreman will buy it. The boxes will be lowered to the path
the women are walking up
as they always did, as they always will now.
Facing the paradox. Learning to die of it.

Exile! Exile!

All night the room breathes out its grief.
Exhales through surfaces. The sideboard.
The curtains. The stale air stalled there.
The kiln-fired claws of the china bird.

This is the hour when every ornament
unloads its atoms of pretence. Stone.
Brass. Bronze. What they represent is
set aside in the dark. They become again

a spacious morning in the Comeraghs.
An iron gate; a sudden downpour; a well in
the corner of a farmyard; a pool of rain
into which an Irish world has fallen.

Out there the Americas stretch to the horizons.
They burn in the cities and darken over wheat.
They go to the edge, to the rock, to the coast,
to where the moon abrades a shabby path eastward.

O land of opportunity, you are
not the suppers with meat, nor
the curtains with lace nor the unheard of
fire in the grate on summer afternoons, you are

this room, this dish of fruit which
has never seen its own earth. Or had rain
fall on it all one night and the next. And has grown,
in consequence, a fine, crazed skin of porcelain.

Once in Dublin

Small things
make the past.
Make the present seem out of place.

A woman cracking and twisting.
Black atoms falling down
on green leaves.

If I am ever to go back
to what I loved first
here are words to be wished on –

(almost, you can see, an incantation).

Summon blue air
out of a corridor between
a mountain range and a sea –

(this at least has never changed).

Empty out the streets.
Fit the cars easily
into their parking places.
Slow the buses down by thirty years.

Observe a brave, fiery shower
above a plate
of bacon and potatoes –

(we are nearly there).

Now say *dinner* for *lunch*.
And *tea-time* instead of *supper*.

And see how it comes again –

My little earth.

My city of white pepper.

How We Made a New Art on Old Ground

A famous battle happened in this valley.
            You never understood the nature poem.
Till now. Till this moment – if these statements
            seem separate, unrelated, follow this

silence to its edge and you will hear
            the history of air: the crispness of a fern
or the upward cut and turn around of
            a fieldfare or thrush written on it.

The other history is silent: the estuary
            is over there. The issue was decided here:
Two kings prepared to give no quarter.
            Then one king and one dead tradition.

Now the humid dusk, the old wounds
            wait for language, for a different truth.
When you see the silk of the willow
            and the wider edge of the river turn

and grow dark and then darker, then
            you will know that the nature poem
is not the action nor its end: it is
            this rust on the gate beside the trees, on

the cattle grid underneath our feet,
            on the steering wheel shaft: it is
an aftermath, an overlay and even, in
            its own modest way, an art of peace:

I try the word *distance* and it fills with
            sycamores, a summer's worth of pollen.
And as I write *valley* straw, metal
            blood, oaths, armour are unwritten.

Silence spreads slowly from these words
            to those ilex trees half in, half out
of shadows falling on the shallow ford
            of the south bank beside Yellow island

as twilight shows how this sweet corrosion
　　　　　begins to be complete: what we see
is what the poem says:
　　　　　evening coming – cattle, cattle-shadows –

and whin bushes and a change of weather
　　　　　about to change them all: what we see is how
the place and the torment of the place are
　　　　　for this moment free of one another.

Emigrant Letters

That morning in Detroit at the airport,
after check-in, heading for the concourse,
I heard, as I was walking towards the gate –
behind me to the left – an Irish voice.

Its owner must have been away for years.
Vowels half-sounds and syllables
from somewhere else had nearly smoothed out
a way of speaking you could tell a region by,

much less an origin. I reached the gate, boarded,
closed my eyes and rose high over
towns, farms, fields – all of them at that very moment
moulding the speech of whoever lived there.

An accent overwritten by a voice. A voice
by a place. Over the waters of the coast
they were entrusted to, trying to think
of loss, I thought of them instead: emigrant letters.

Every word told and re-told.
Handed over, held close, longed-for and feared.
Each page six crisp inches of New England snow.
And at the end a name: half signature, half salt.

How their readers stood in cold kitchens
heads bent, until the time came to begin again
folding over those chambers of light:
ice and owl-noise and the crystal freight on

branches and fences, and added them
to the stitchwort of late spring, then mosquitoes,
the unheard of heat, the wild leaves, snow again –
the overnight disappearance of wood and stone –

all of which they stored side by side
carefully in a cupboard drawer which never
would close properly: informed as it was
by those distant seasons. And warped by its own.

The Burdens of a History

I

I have a reason for remembering
the unseasonable heat of that evening.

A skin of wet air on the apples.
The plane tree leaves dry as lavender.

II

We said we would not talk about the past:
About what had happened. (Which is history.)
About what could happen. (Which is fear.)

III

Then you brought a map down from the attic,
folded in such a way it fell open
at once in your hands and had the feel
of linen partly. And paper only slightly.

These were wetlands. This was the coast.
This was our country. And already
the spidery red lines were widening
into the roads our parents drove west on

looking for signposts they had just missed.

IV

I went into a field above the city
when I was just fourteen years of age.

Before sex, before settling down,
before growing up, there was this:

Rust was everywhere, a second skin
on every inch of iron.
Distances were less ambitious.
Car parts and wheels in the ditches
seemed to say that travel was an error
whose starting point would end back here.

In this air made out of humid blues.
And the cattle which had not moved once.

V

When the storm broke they were under it.
The heat cracking. Rain hissing on the car.

They counted from the thunder on their fingers.
And waited in the freshening, lifting air
for the first strike of lightning which –
if it did not kill them –

would show them exactly where they were.

Horace Odes: II:XI

Don't worry about it Quinctius. Don't fret.
Whatever they plan, the Cantabrians and the Scythians –
Divided from us by the Adriatic Sea –
    signifies almost nothing. Life is short.

And asks little of us. How soon the bright
days of our youth and beauty end and old age
puts paid to love and ease, not to mention the gift
    of going out like a light.

The wildflowers of spring will not inherit
the earth forever nor the moon shine like this.
Why do you weary yourself? Why do you worry
    the infinite question with your finite spirit?

Why not drink this wine under the high, airy
plane trees and pines while we can, our greying hair
garlanded with rose leaves and fragrant with
    the sweet oils and balsam of Syria?

For the god of wine is the enemy of care.
And which slave-boy will bring us water now
from the passing stream to cool down and temper
    our bowls of Falernian fire?

And as for Lyde, who is going to persuade her,
shy as she is, to leave home and join us? Tell her to hurry.
Tell her to come, dressed Laconian-style, with
    her ivory lyre and her hair neatly tied.

     NEW COLLECTED POEMS

Echo

after Pushkin

After the sound of an animal howling.
After the thunder. After the horn.
After the song of a mountain woman
There is silence and empty air.
Then you are there.

You listen. The thunder calls.
You listen. The waves are speaking.
You answer. But no one will ever
Answer you. And you know it.
And the same is true for you

– poet!

Hide this Place from Angels

Tinderbox weather. Even the whins were on fire.
At dusk the ground was hard and the air dried.
A single star rose over the charred
garden hedges and whitebeams of our neighbourhood.

Tinderbox faith. Those centuries in the dark:
the sinner's moving lips and patient look –
the syllables seeking a miracle –
dried to kindling: waiting in drought and silence for a spark.

August. High summer in an Irish town.
Tied sheaves and a sea haze near the ocean.
A stature of the Virgin: a passerby at her shrine
who sees her move, who sees her step down: let the blaze begin

and continue: In Ballinspittle and Kinsale
men watched as the impossible became believable,
as virgins ceased to be unavailable,
as they wept real tears under sky-blue creases and plaster veils.

I lived far away. When the sun rose over
the suburb with its slate roofs and leaf cover
news came in of a season of heat and fever
no one could remember happening before in those parts: not ever.

I leaned on the windowsill. The sky was still light.
The air had heat in it and some dew and soon the weight
of the lives we lived would become inert
house and tree shadows: odd simulacra of a summer quiet.

South of me where the roots of the lilac had died
where fuchsia hung down over stone walls on the road
waiting for salt, waiting for rain, I understood
how deep they went – those thirsts that could not be satisfied.

And should have felt them, should have entered them. Instead
I stood at the open window: hide this place I said
from angels. From the terrible regard
of those who come to find them, shelter it.

I watched the tops of the Dublin hills burn out
all evening and the helicopters with their iron freight
and tonnage of water drop down what was not
the wild rain they had failed to imitate.

Limits 2

If there was
a narrative to my life
in those years, then
let this
be the sound of it –
the season, in, season out
sound of
the grind of
my neighbours' shears.

Beautiful air of August,
music of limitation, of
the clipped
shadow and
the straightened border,
of rain on the Dublin hills,
of my children sleeping in
a simpler world:
an iron edge
the origin of order.

How the Earth and All the Planets Were Created

I went to find the grave of my grandmother
who died before my time. And hers.

I searched among marsh grass and granite
and single headstones
and smashed lettering
and archangel wings and found none.

For once I said
I will face this landscape
and look at it as she was looked upon:

Unloved because unknown.
Unknown because un-named:

Glass Pistol Castle disappeared.
Baltray and then Clogher Head.

To the west the estuary of the Boyne –
stripped of its battles and history –
became only willow-trees and distances.

I drove back in the half light
of late summer on
anonymous roads on my journey home
as the constellations rose overhead,
some of them twisted into women:

pinioned and winged
and single-handedly holding high the dome
and curve and horizon of today and tomorrow.

All the ships looking up to them.
All the compasses made true by them.
All the night skies named for their sorrow.

A Model Ship Made by Prisoners Long Ago

There it is my father said.

He put it down beside
the stack of coins
and the brass striking clock
on the mantelpiece.

A ship:
Made of parchment,
of canvas. Of foraged-for
crude glues.

Your great-grandfather
joined the Tipperary Horse.
He rose to be head of the Poorhouse.
That is, Master of the Union.

On the mantelpiece
a snipe is flying across a florin,
its base-metal wing lost to its destination
of wetlands and crab-grass.

He had fourteen children.
Eight of them survived.
He educated every one of them.
Some of them were women.

In the dark, in the stone-cold,
their fingers had threaded, moulded,
made the foc'sle, the hull,
then the spar and the rigging
and the promise of
a billowing main sail.

As if they could
still breathe phosphor and starlight
they had made it: their need for freedom
only visible
in what they missed.

No porpoises making a circle
of light and muscle.
No Pole Star.
No discernible line of landfall.

Is It Still the Same

young woman who climbs the stairs,
who closes a child's door,
who goes to her table
in a room at the back of a house?
The same unlighted corridor?
The same night air
over the wheelbarrows and rain-tanks?
The same inky sky and pin-bright stars?
You can see nothing of her, but her head
bent over the page, her hand moving,
moving again, and her hair.
I wrote like that once.
But this is different.
This time, when she looks up, I will be there.

Suburban Woman: Another Detail

Dusk.
        And the neighbourhood
is the colour of shadow,
the colour of stone:

Here at my desk I imagine
wintry air and the smart of peat.

And an uncurtained
front room where

another woman is living my life.
Another woman is lifting my child.

Is setting her down.
Is cutting oily rind from a lemon.
Is crushing that smell against the skin of her fingers.

She goes to my door and closes it.
Goes to my window and pulls the curtain slowly.

The kitchen,
the child she lifts again and holds
are all mine:
                        and all the time
the bitter, citric fragrance stays against her skin.

She stares at the road
in the featureless November twilight.

Stares for a moment at
the moon which has drained it.

Then pulls the curtains tightly shut.
And puts herself and my child beyond it.

Irish Poetry

for Michael Hartnett

We always knew there was no Orpheus in Ireland.
No music stored at the doors of hell.
No god to make it.
No wild beasts to weep and lie down to it.

But I remember an evening when the sky
was underworld-dark at four,
when ice had seized every part of the city
and we sat talking –
the air making a wreath for our cups of tea.

And you began to speak of our own gods.
Our heartbroken pantheon.

No Attic light for them and no Herodotus.
But thin rain and dogfish and the stopgap
of the sharp cliffs
they spent their winters on.

And the pitch-black Atlantic night.
How the sound
of a bird's wing in a lost language sounded.

You made the noise for me.
Made it again.
Until I could see the flight of it: suddenly

the silvery lithe rivers of the south-west
lay down in silence
and the savage acres no one could predict
were all at ease, soothed and quiet and

listening to you, as I was. As if to music, as if to peace.

Index of First Lines

INDEX OF FIRST LINES

Index of Titles